MARBLEHEAD
IN
WORLD WAR I

MARBLEHEAD

I N

WORLD WAR I

AT HOME & OVERSEAS

MARGERY A. ARMSTRONG

Charleston London

THE
History
PRESS

Published by The History Press
Charleston, SC 29403
www.historypress.net

Front cover, top: Tenth Deck Band. *Courtesy of Marblehead Historical Commission, Abbot Hall,
Marblehead, MA, object ID 1961-001-02387. www.marbleheadhistory.com.*
Back cover, top left: Ezekiel Russell Peach in World War I uniform. *Courtesy of Zeke R. Peach Jr.;*
top right: Members of the Tenth Deck Division on USS *Nebraska*, Charlestown Navy Yard,
Charlestown, MA. *Courtesy of Marblehead Historical Commission, Abbot Hall, Marblehead, MA,
object ID 1961-001-00641. www.marbleheadhistory.com.*

First published 2011
Manufactured in the United States
ISBN 978.1.60949.149.9

Library of Congress Cataloging-in-Publication Data
Armstrong, Margery A.
Marblehead in World War I : at home and overseas / Margery A. Armstrong.
p. cm.
Includes bibliographical references and index.
ISBN 978-1-60949-149-9
1. World War, 1914-1918--Massachusetts--Marblehead. 2. World War, 1914-1918--Social
aspects--Massachusetts--Marblehead. 3. Marblehead (Mass.)--History, Military--20th
century. 4. Marblehead (Mass.)--Social conditions--20th century. 5. Community
life--Massachusetts--Marblehead--History--20th century. 6. Soldiers--Massachusetts--
Marblehead--Biography. 7. Marblehead (Mass.)--Biography. I. Title. II. Title: Marblehead
in World War 1. III. Title: Marblehead in World War One.
D570.85.M41M272 2011
940.3'7445--dc22
2011010589

Dedicated to my mother and grandmother who always told me "you can accomplish whatever you want as long as you set your mind to it."

"Marblehead Forever"
By Reverend Marcia M. Selman
Sung to the tune of "The Lily of the Valley"

The men of old were heroes,
who fought by land and sea,
To preserve their homes
from tyranny and shame;
And, enrolled among the bravest,
writ high in history,
Stands old Marblehead's beloved and honored name.

Chorus:
Then Marblehead Forever!
God bless the good old town!
May she never shame her noble ancestry!
She was first in Revolution, was first in '61,
And from whiskey bondage we will keep her free!

The men of old were heroes,
but they are in their graves,
And 'tis ours, their sons,
the battle now to fight,
For our homes and altars tremble,
before the greed of knaves,
Who assail the cause of God and home and right.

Then Marblehead Forever!
God bless the good old town!
May she never shame her noble ancestry!
She was first in Revolution, was first in '61,
And from whiskey bondage we will keep her free!

Then up and do your duty!
Too long ingloriously,
Did we sleep while rum held

Undisputed sway.
Now rally with your ballots,
And let his hirelings see,
That when we first drove him out he went to stay.

Then Marblehead Forever!
God bless the good old town!
May she never shame her noble ancestry!
She was first in Revolution, was first in '61,
And from whiskey bondage we will keep her free!

CONTENTS

ACKNOWLEDGEMENTS

I would like to offer my thanks and appreciation to the people and organizations that have assisted me in my first writing venture. First my husband, Paul, for locating microfilm of the *Marblehead Messenger* and putting it on CDs so I could research to my heart's content in the comfort of my own home. A special thank-you to Pam Peterson of the Marblehead Historical Society for suggesting I submit my work to The History Press, and to my editors, Jeff Saraceno and Hilary McCullough, and the entire staff at The History Press for making this venture happen. Thank you to Chris Johnson and Wayne Butler of the Marblehead Historical Commission for assisting me in locating images and for scanning the images for my use. Thank you to Clifford Brown Sr., Ezekiel R. Peach Jr. and Maureen Graves Anderson for sharing World War I memorabilia from their family collections. Finally, a thank-you to my colleague Deborah Stewart for proofreading this work and giving me a boost of confidence.

My biggest thanks to my mother and father, William and Barbara Taylor, who provided me with the opportunity to grow up in such a great and historical town as Marblehead; and to all my ancestors in town who started me on this genealogical and writing quest. Finally, thank you to all my friends and family who have had to listen to me talking about my book for several years.

INTRODUCTION

W hy did I decide to write about these particular years in Marblehead's history? It all started when I began researching my extensive Marblehead ancestry. Marbleheaders are all familiar with their names—Martin, Bessom, Roundy, Freeto, Smith, Foss, Devereux, Woodfin, Peach and the list goes on and on. I was searching on eBay and came across a gentleman from Iowa who was selling a bound version of the 1918 *Marblehead Messenger*. I had to have it; microfilm readers cause too much motion sickness. I was lucky enough to win the auction. From there, I became engrossed with reading these old papers. They hold a wealth of information, not only on my relatives but also on the comings and goings of the whole town.

The years 1914 through 1919 were the years of World War I. Although the United States did not officially enter the war until 1917, its preparation for the war began several years before this. Never being much of a history buff in the past, I was fascinated with the letters the soldiers wrote home to their families telling what they could of their experiences in the war. There were also weekly accountings of how the town prepared for the war. From reading these newspapers, I was intrigued with how much involvement the community had in the affairs of the times. There were celebrations to send soldiers off to war and celebrations when they returned, and many hardworking committees were set up to serve the needs of the soldiers overseas as well as their families at home. The Burgess Aeroplane factory was used during this time for government contracts for warplanes. The Tenth Deck Division of the Naval Militia was commissioned in Marblehead, and training camps were set up on Marblehead Neck to train men for coastal patrols.

There was such a sense of community in those times; I felt it was worth noting. I also felt that originals of these letters have probably been lost or tossed away and that families and friends of those Marblehead boys who served in the military may want to experience what their ancestors endured during World War I. I have chosen in some instances to use only excerpts from their letters but have noted in the notes where you can find the full content of the letter on the microfilm of the *Marblehead Messenger*, available at Abbot Public Library in Marblehead, Massachusetts. I read many letters and chose ones that I felt held the best information to portray what life was like in the military and the flavor of Marblehead. No editing was done on the letters and excerpts; it represents the language and style of the time. I apologize to any family members who had letters from relatives in the service that did not get mentioned in this book. There were so many published in the *Messenger*, and I only had a small amount of space in which to use them.

I hope you enjoy this work as I truly enjoyed researching and writing it.

Chapter 1

MARBLEHEAD PREPARES FOR WAR

PATRIOTISM

World War I, the First World War, the Great War and the War to End All Wars—all describe the global military conflict that took place from 1914 to 1919 involving the majority of the world's great powers. Over seventy million military personnel were mobilized in one of the largest wars in history. As usual, Marblehead played its part in this Great War, as it had in all of America's previous wars.

This book is not about the world politics that contributed to the war but rather how a small seacoast town in Massachusetts once again did its part in honoring America and its soldiers. Much of the information for this book has come from the reporters for the local newspaper, the *Marblehead Messenger*. I have chosen to use much of the same text as was described in these news reports and letters from the soldiers to their loved ones at home as a means of reflecting the language and writing style of the early twentieth century.

Anyone from Marblehead knows that it is the birthplace of the American navy and was first to answer Lincoln's call for soldiers in the Civil War. What you may not know is that Marblehead was one of the first municipalities to begin preparing for World War I when, in 1915, town officials proposed to the federal government that the town should have a naval militia. After all, Marblehead is a seaport town, and the men and boys have experience on the high seas. This would come to be known as the Tenth Deck Division of the Naval Militia.

Marblehead first began preparing for war with an old-fashioned mass meeting of the townsfolk held at Abbot Hall on Tuesday night, November 30, 1915, at eight o'clock. It was here that the townsmen met to make all the people of the town aware of the urgent need of patriotic preparedness against foreign invasion. This portion of Massachusetts was ideal for an enemy invasion due to the number of cotton mills, woolen mills, shoe factories, ammunition factories, powder magazines, aero-plane shops and almost everything an army would find useful in a time of war.

Mr. Chester L. Dane, who later joined the Marblehead Naval Militia, was chairman of the meeting, which completely filled the auditorium of Abbot Hall. Mr. Eliot Wadsworth of the Rockefeller War Relief Foundation was the first to speak to the people and told of his recent experience in Europe touring the war zone. He told of how he toured through Austria and was amazed that the military had not been properly drilled, showed no organization and was imperfectly led; as a result, sixty-five thousand soldiers were taken prisoner during the attack against Servia. On the other hand, the Turkish army, which had a payroll of twenty cents per man and a ration of two pounds of bread daily, had been training for many years and, as a result, was able to hold the highly equipped English army in the Gallipoli peninsula for six months.[1] He told the men and women that "the United States needed more of a navy and especially more men trained to serve intelligently in the time of need." He urged the Americans to start training now, "as it takes time to make soldiers out of citizens."

Colonel Frank A. Graves of Marblehead was the last speaker of the evening and told of the contest between Marblehead and Newburyport for the award of having a naval brigade formed in the town. Newburyport won the first round because it mustered up more enthusiasm. On inspection night, forty-eight men showed up in Marblehead and seventy-eight in Newburyport. He explained there was one more company to be commissioned and it was between Marblehead and Gloucester. He reminded the audience of the "priceless heritage of Marblehead in the deeds of their noble ancestors." He urged all the young men of the town to come and join. The first young man in the audience to respond was Mr. Preston N. Lincoln of Boston, ensign of Company B of the Naval Militia in Boston. He was quickly followed by a large number of Marbleheaders, the total reaching nearly ninety.

Postcard of Abbot Hall in Marblehead, Massachusetts, location of patriotic mass meetings. *Author's collection.*

Postcard of Abbot Hall. *Author's collection.*

Tenth Deck Division

The Naval Militia was Marblehead's first step in its preparedness. Any male desiring to become a member could sign enlistment papers available in town at the plumbing supply store of Ernest S. Doane. Once a sufficient number had enlisted, the request was sent to the State Naval Board to have it assign a company of 54 men to the town. By December 1915, there were 130 names on the enlistment papers. The board then gave each man a physical examination and administered, to those who qualified, the primary oath of allegiance.

On December 24, 1915, the application was approved, and Marblehead was granted a Naval Militia unit. Governor David Walsh signed the official paper on December 31, 1915. In total, there were fifteen Naval Militia companies in Massachusetts, ten deck companies and five signal companies. The company assigned to Marblehead was Deck Company No. 10 or, as the

Old Marblehead Academy and Armory, Pleasant Street, Marblehead. *Courtesy of Marblehead Historical Commission, Abbot Hall, Marblehead, MA object ID 1961-001-00173. www. marbleheadhistory.com.*

Members of the Tenth Deck Division on USS *Nebraska*, Charlestown Navy Yard, Charlestown, Massachusetts. *Courtesy of Marblehead Historical Commission, Abbot Hall, Marblehead, MA, object ID 1961-001-00641. www.marbleheadhistory.com.*

Members of the Tenth Deck Division, Marblehead. *Courtesy of Marblehead Historical Commission, Abbot Hall, Marblehead, MA, object ID 1961-001-01933. www.marbleheadhistory.com.*

Members of the Tenth Deck Division, Marblehead. *Courtesy of Marblehead Historical Commission, Abbot Hall, Marblehead, MA, object ID 1961-001- 01934. www.marbleheadhistory.com.*

Tenth Deck Band. *Courtesy of Marblehead Historical Commission, Abbot Hall, Marblehead, MA, object ID 1961-001- 02387. www.marbleheadhistory.com.*

Entire Tenth Deck Division. *Courtesy of Marblehead Historical Commission, Abbot Hall, Marblehead, MA, object ID 1961-002-03390. www.marbleheadhistory.com.*

town referred to it, the Tenth Deck Division. Its men later became known as the National Naval Volunteers of Marblehead, Massachusetts.[2]

This was the fifth and last militia company in Marblehead's history to be sent into combat, being dissolved at the end of the war. (See the appendix for the full roster of the Tenth Deck Division.)

TRAINING BEGINS

The Marblehead men wasted no time in beginning their training and were formally mustered into service on January 16, 1916. Chester L. Dane was elected chief, Greely S. Curtis was lieutenant and Ernest S. Doane was ensign. After passing the required examinations, the officers officially took command of the unit in March 1916. During the interim, Commander Robinson from the State Militia was in charge of the training.

Every Monday night, with the exception of the yearly Monday night town meeting, the men gathered for drills at Abbot Hall. There was some concern regarding the marching drills that took place. They could only be held on the ground floor, as the steady steps of marching tended to set the whole building swaying. In May 1916, it was decided to move all the drills to the Academy Building on Pleasant Street, originally the old high school. The heating system in the Academy Building was totally inadequate for the men and necessitated that the members dress in their uniforms at home or risk catching a cold. Along with the marching drills, the division was broken up into squads and instructed in naval etiquette and signals.

During February and March 1916, the government began shipping supplies to the town for the men to use in their drills. The first to arrive was a four-inch gun, a new gun in the United States' arsenal, and was the type used on the deck of cruisers and in the secondary batteries of battleships. It was ten feet in length and weighed three and a half tons. Delivered by train to the freight house in town, it sat for months at a cost to the government of a dollar a day, until it was finally set up in the large room on the first floor of the Academy Building. A new twelve-oared cutter was also delivered and was moored in the harbor at the John S. Martin coal wharf for the men to practice on.

Throughout the spring of 1916, regular inspections of the company and its drills were performed by the Naval Board, and the Marblehead men always passed with flying colors. They received a ranking of five, a perfect score.

First Taste of the Sea

The U.S. government made arrangements for a torpedo boat destroyer to come from the Charlestown Navy Yard to Marblehead Harbor on Saturday, May 6, 1916, at which time part of the Tenth Deck Division went aboard and spent the night. Although most of the men were used to life on boats, this gave the division its first taste of actual saltwater conditions on a torpedo boat. One of the first journeys the division took was to Provincetown, during which a number of "stunts" were tried. The men from Marblehead were found to be very apt in taking hold of the maneuvers, especially for such a new and young company. The destroyer arrived back in the harbor with a tired, dirty but well-pleased division and no case of mal de mar reported. Several more training missions were held on this torpedo boat, as well as the battleship *Nebraska*.

Orders Received

Training ended on July 25, 1916, when word was received that the Tenth Deck Division had to report for its tour of duty on the USS *Kearsarge*[3] on Tuesday, August 11, 1916. On that morning, the men gathered in full uniform at the armory and marched up to the train station on Pleasant Street, where they took the eight o'clock train to Boston, arriving at North Station. From there, they fell in and marched to the Charlestown Navy Yard, where they embarked on the USS *Kearsarge*. Adjutant General Eldridge was overheard saying that "the Marblehead Company was the finest that he had seen."[4]

Quite a number of Marblehead's townsfolk took the train to Boston to see the men off, and it was a source of pride for everyone who watched them. As quoted in the *Marblehead Messenger* on August 15, 1916, "It demonstrated that the old spirit of the town was not dead and by its preparedness its youth may be depended upon once again to respond in time of need as in the days of yore."

From the Charlestown Navy Yard, the cruise took the men to Portland, Maine, where members of the Maine Naval Militia joined the vessel. From Portland, they set sail to Provincetown, Massachusetts, where they were headquartered. They practiced maneuvers intended to familiarize them with the practical operations of the battleship. This was the first time they were in competition with other deck divisions, and they earned the praise of all the officers for their seamanship and gentlemanly conduct at all times. In the regular drills and practice, they were given the highest percentage of any of the divisions onboard, and a trophy cup was sent to the Marblehead Armory as visible evidence of their hard work.

Upon their return to Marblehead, they were given a royal welcome at the train station, where the drum corps was waiting for them. Following an impromptu reception, the drum corps led the sailors on a march around town and back to the armory, where they disbanded.

AVIATION DIVISION

Following the ruling of the Naval Board, along with a naval division there also had to be an aviation section having twelve men attached to it. Mr. Greely S. Curtis had been actively engaged in promoting this section, which was the first aviation section on the Atlantic Coast and the second in the country. As most of the Marblehead boys were seafaring, the naval division was much more appealing to them than aviation; however, they were able to complete the requirements of having an aviation division. Norman W.

Cabot was ensign, and the crew members were George R. Fearing Jr., Bayard Tuckerman Jr., Gordon Balch and Clifford L. Webster. These four men purchased an airplane known as the Cabot to use for training purposes.

The aviation division was mustered into service on June 5, 1916, and the men began their two-week tour of duty with an encampment on Misery Island, off the coast of Beverly, Massachusetts, on Wednesday, September 13, 1916. Misery Island was chosen as a training area because of its accessibility as well as the proximity to the Burgess plant of the Curtis Aeroplane Works in Marblehead. The water was generally calm in this area, as it was protected by a chain of islands and reefs. The men were housed in tents, and any equipment that was needed was shipped by road from Boston and transported by the Tenth Deck Division's rowing cutter to the island. It was a regular military camp for the purpose of drilling the men in flying and signaling.

One afternoon during training, in view of the cottages located along the west shore of Marblehead, one of the Burgess-Dunne aero-planes fell into the waters of Salem Harbor. Aviator McGrath was teaching George F. Fearing by having him shut off the power at a height of nearly a half mile and then proceed into a steep spiral descent. When nearly down, McGrath signaled Fearing what to do, but Fearing misinterpreted the signals, and the plane struck the water rather heavily, slightly damaging one wing. The occupants were shaken up but otherwise unharmed, and the aero-plane was towed to the Burgess plant, where it was discarded.[5]

CALL TO ARMS

In late March 1917, an order was received from the government for the men of the Tenth Deck Division to pack up their kits and be available to leave on short notice. The country was preparing to enter World War I. A large patriotic demonstration by the townsfolk was held on a Sunday evening at Abbot Hall, and the division was presented their colors. Mr. Theodore P. Day, known as "Daddy" of the Tenth Deck Division, had told the citizens a few weeks before that it was only fitting that they make a contribution and purchase the men a set of colors. He started the fund by offering up one dollar, and the town was canvassed for additional funds. On that Sunday evening, the hall was overflowing with twenty-five hundred townspeople, including hundreds of women and children. Many had to be turned away but remained outside the building to show their support. Promptly at 7:30 p.m., the Tenth Deck Division, in command of Lieutenant Chester L. Dane, headed by the Harris Band (a local town band), marched from the armory on Pleasant Street to Abbot Hall. From there they were escorted into the hall by members of the John Goodwin Jr. Post of the Grand Army of the Republic, the Women's Relief Corp, Clarence L. Bartol Camp, William D. Gregory Camp, Sons of Veterans, Mary E. Graves Auxiliary and other town fraternal organizations. There, patriotic speeches were given and the schoolchildren sang patriotic songs. The children also presented the men with a flag they had purchased by collecting their nickels and dimes. Of course, no gathering would be complete without the singing of "Marblehead Forever" by all the townspeople.

On Thursday, March 29, 1917, at 6:45 p.m., the fire whistle blew 4-4-4 to alert the company to report to the armory and receive their orders. Within minutes, the streets were filled with citizens hurrying to the scene to see what was going on. The response of the naval boys to the armory was prompt, as

USS *Nebraska*, sea home of Marblehead's Tenth Deck Division, April 1, 1917. *Photo from Live Wire Committee publication, circa 1919.*

they had been practicing this maneuver for a while. After roll call was taken, the order was read to them that they would report on April 2, 1917, to begin duty on the USS *Nebraska*.[6] They were instructed to return home and make all their necessary preparations and to report back on Friday evening for further instructions. The town now took on a military look as armed guards were placed around the armory.

Prominent citizens of the town met on that Friday evening with the selectmen to adopt plans for another mass meeting the following evening. Their goal was to ensure that the division was suitably equipped when leaving for duty and that their families would be cared for during their absence. Their biggest concern was in supplying the men with warm underclothing and winter wear. There was a lot of discussion about the monetary collections that would be needed to provide for these families. One generous gentleman, Mr. Herbert Humphrey, agreed to make up the difference out of his own pocket between the collection at the mass meeting and the expenses incurred. Mr. Theodore P. Day reminded the selectmen that he believed in giving the boys a splendid sendoff with music and parades; money would be needed for such affairs. In total, about $2,500 had been contributed during the mass meeting to the Military Relief Fund, according to Treasurer Everett Paine. Most families donated $1 each, with the names of those donors printed in the local newspaper. (My great-grandfather, Clinton Foss, was one of the many contributors.)

On Palm Sunday morning, April 1, 1917, as was to be expected, the men departed town with a lot of fanfare. The booming of the cannons and the tolling of the church bells—which began promptly at 9:15 a.m. and continued for half an hour—could be heard throughout the town. This was the fifth time in the history of the town that military organizations had gone forth to defend the honor of Old Glory. The men assembled at the armory at 8:00 a.m., and their baggage was loaded on the Woodfin Brothers' biggest automobile truck and left for Charlestown ahead of them. The men, led by Police Officers Reuben Paine, John Collyer, Clinton Foss and John Gilbert, marched from the armory to Bank Square (Washington Street), where they were met by nearly fifty automobiles, all decorated with American flags, donated and driven by the men of the town. They stopped to have their pictures taken by photographers Fred B. Litchman and F. Thompson at the post office on Pleasant Street. They were then driven up Front Street to

Washington to Pleasant Street and out of town to Monument Square in Chelsea, Massachusetts. From there they marched to the Charlestown Navy Yard, as they had practiced in their drills, and boarded the USS *Nebraska*. All along the route friends, families and townspeople were out on the streets and in their doorways waving flags as a farewell to the men. Upon arrival on board ship, the men were served a meal of fried veal cutlets, stewed corn, mashed potatoes, bread and butter, mince pie and coffee. The division was mustered into the United States service as national naval volunteers and would begin serving their country.

Thanks to the preparedness of Marblehead, the men left town well equipped in regard to training, clothing and supplies. In fact, they were so well equipped that for days the men had the record of being the only command of militia to enter Charlestown Navy Yard with a proper supply of clothing. They were each given two suits of heavy underclothing, a sweater, muffler, hose, wristers, gloves and a helmet, as well as two hand towels, one bath towel, one face towel and six handkerchiefs.

Not long after their departure, the town received a letter from Herman F. Snow from the USS *Nebraska* telling the town:

> *We are on a fine ship and have the best of everything. We are starting to have a meeting of all the boys each night so we can keep track of each other. Under the present system we cannot see our own members, except by chance meetings. We are divided into different watches and messes which makes the probability of seeing each other complicated.*[7]

The duty assignment of the USS *Nebraska* developed into maneuvers, battle practice, drills and exercises with the Atlantic Fleet. In May 1917, a letter was received from Commander Chester L. Dane urging the townspeople to send gifts to the boys.

> *Dear Old Friends—*
>
> *Just a word for you and our friends, which to me means everyone in Marblehead. Your boys have dropped into the United States Navy and are now doing great work. Almost without exception they are praised and respected for the fine way of preparing their difficult tasks and they are difficult; this war is not a cruise and things are fast getting on a war basis.*

A number of times I have heard this remark, "He is a good man, he comes from Marblehead, from the best division on board." I am proud of them. They are still my children and come to me for advice and aid the same way they did at home. If they stick to it, the future generations will be proud of the Tenth Deck Division. I cannot give you any real details of our life, but am saving them for you. Give my best regards to all and tell them that we are on the job and are doing our bit with all our strengths.[8]

The town rallied after reading this letter, and the Express Wagon was loaded with four hundred pounds of supplies for the boys. This was a group effort by the town, and the gifts began arriving at Abbot Hall to be sent to the boys. What to do with the supplies was a problem, and Mr. Michael C. Grady was called upon to assist packing the gifts, as he had nine years' experience in the shipping room of a large factory. After all the parcels were packed, it was noted that five boys had not been remembered, so the men pooled what change they had in their pockets and came up with enough to buy each boy cigars, cigarettes and two pounds of candy. Word was received from the boys that the packages were received and shared with their shipmates.

The "Nebby," as it was called, became a training ship for armed guard gun crews during the winter of 1917. It was then assigned to a special mission in 1918 going to Montevideo, Uruguay, and then joined the Atlantic convoy trips to France. By this time, the boys from Marblehead were scattered on various battleships seeing service on any one of the seven seas depending on their rank and experience.

According to Jack Clark of the USS *Nebraska*, life was not too bad on the ship but not like home: "We have moving pictures three times a week. It is Saturday afternoon and while many in Marblehead are enjoying the ball games (at Seaside Park) we are at anchor writing letters. We enjoy singing and occasionally have boxing on board."[9]

An entertaining letter dated October 2, 1917, was received from Edward H. Caswell Jr., bugler on the USS *Nebraska*. He reported that all of the Marblehead boys who remained on the *Nebraska* were well, but they missed the "hearty infectious laugh" of Williard Roach, who was transferred from the ship. They also missed the presence of William Woodfin, who was serving on the USS *Richmond*.[10]

March 1918 was the one-year anniversary of the Tenth Deck Division leaving town, and so far no one had perished, for which the town was grateful. They did lose one man in the war, George Morrill of Swampscott, who died at the Naval Hospital in Gibraltar. Following the end of the war, the former members of the Tenth Deck Division formed a temporary organization in Marblehead designed to keep alive the bond the men had formed.

Chapter 2

MARBLEHEAD FACTORIES
AID THE GOVERNMENT

THE BURGESS COMPANY

Even the town industries and workers were affected by the war efforts, some favorable and some not. One Marblehead company that played a large role in the war was the Burgess plant, owned by Mr. W. Sterling Burgess, a 1901 Harvard University graduate. After completing courses in special engineering and naval architecture, he followed in the steps of his father as a naval architect. He was so successful that within a very short time his offices were moved from Boston to Salem, Massachusetts, where he started the first Burgess Yacht Yard. This plant soon proved to be too small, and with the growth of his business, the No. 1 Plant was purchased in Marblehead on Redstone Lane near Tucker's Wharf. For a number of years, this plant was devoted entirely to the construction of fast sailing and motor craft of his design. He then became interested in aeronautics at the same time the Wright brothers were achieving success in Ohio. He designed and constructed a number of experimental machines in conjunction with Mr. Greely S. Curtis of Boston, testing them at Plum Island. They proved so successful that the United States Army placed contracts with the Burgess Company for airplanes in 1911, those being among the first regular requisitions for aircraft in our military service. From then on, the business grew steadily, and in 1915, a combat machine of Mr. Burgess's design was produced at the request of the British admiralty and shipped to England.[11]

Burgess Plant #1, Redstone Lane, Marblehead. *Courtesy of Marblehead Historical Commission, Abbot Hall, Marblehead, MA, object ID 1961-002- 03200.* www.marbleheadhistory.com.

The first order they received from the United States government was in November 1916 for Burgess tractor land machines (hydroplanes). Mr. Burgess himself designed these low-powered flying machines, which were to be used as teaching planes for soldiers. Up until this time, the United States had virtually neglected the aviation portion of fighting the war. Business became so brisk for Mr. Burgess that he needed to build a newer, more modern factory.

PLANT No. 2

Burgess chose the site of his second plant in Marblehead to be on Gas House Lane, Little Harbor, on land formerly belonging to the Lynn Gas and Electric Company and by the Marblehead Gas Company. This second building was built of steel and brick construction, the size being three hundred by one hundred feet at a cost of $60,000. This building was to be used for assembling the airplanes while the parts were being made at the Redstone Lane plant. To facilitate the launching of the planes at Plant

No. 2, the end of the building facing the water was made so that it could be opened, allowing the planes to be taken in and out of the factory on the tracks that were constructed for this purpose. At that time, the plant was the second largest in the country.

The contract for the steel to build the new building was given to the Ferguson Steel and Iron Company of Buffalo, New York, which had built another plant for the Curtis Company in Buffalo. Much of the actual construction of the plant was sublet to local contractors in Marblehead. The Woodfin Brothers Express Company completed one of its biggest trucking contracts by hauling the two hundred tons of structural steel from the railway station to Gas House Lane. Due to the harsh winter of 1917, this was done entirely by horse teams over icy and snowy street conditions. Contractor Thomas D. Snow of Marblehead began work on the plant on January 9, 1917, and the building was in use by April 27, 1917. With the addition of the second factory, Burgess needed to increase the number of men he employed, and Marblehead men were given first preference.

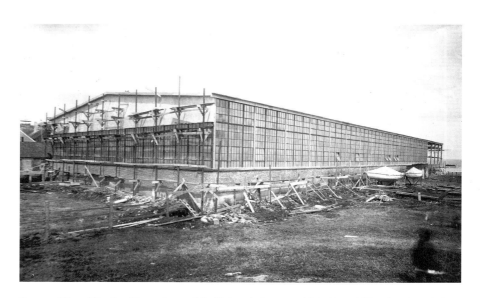

Burgess Plant #2, Gas House Lane, Marblehead. *Courtesy of Marblehead Historical Commission, Abbot Hall, Marblehead, MA, object ID 1961-002-03201. www.marbleheadhistory.com.*

STANDING GUARD

Due to the nature of what was manufactured by the Burgess Company, both plants were heavily guarded both day and night. Former Marblehead patrolmen William Ward and Mr. Graves were employed as guards, as well as a force of eight to ten special policemen of the town. Later, the state militia—composed of a detail of eleven men from Company K, Ninth Regiment, from Clinton, Massachusetts, under the command of Sergeant R.T. Taylor, including a corporal and nine privates—was in charge of protecting the plant. The men were quartered at the Marblehead Catholic Club in one of its rooms on Gregory Street, as conditions were not acceptable at the Burgess plant. The men received their meals at a restaurant in Marblehead that was contracted by the government to provide for the men. In May 1917, after completion of the plant, the militia got ready to leave their patrol. "We are sorry to leave Marblehead, as we have had a pretty good time here and the work was not very hard, not nearly as hard as some of the other men have had guarding railroad bridges and the like. The people in town have been more than kind to us, we really hate to leave," is the way one of the officers described his duty.[12]

WORK BEGINS

In late April 1917, the new plant was completed enough to allow the manufacturing of the planes to begin. Stock was shipped to the site, and work began. Marblehead freight agent Arthur S. Adams was prepared to ship these planes on short notice to wherever the government requested. Planes were shipped almost daily; therefore, the freight cars had to be available for the job, necessitating some runs from Marblehead to other towns be suspended. Other obstacles, such as the strike of the Industrial Workers of the World (IWW) in the West, tied up the lumber mills that produced a good deal of the wood used for these planes.

In January 1918, the government called for a push on airplane production, with the need for the greatest number of machines in the shortest possible time. This pushed the Burgess plant to its limit, measured only by its ability to get the materials and the men for the work. By this time, many of the

Burgess airplane manufactured in Marblehead. *Courtesy of Library of Congress.*

employees and Marblehead men had enlisted in the army, causing a shortage of workers. Nonetheless, they began shipping ten planes a week from their plant, resulting in the need for an addition to be put on Plant No. 2 at Gas House Lane. Even with the addition of ten thousand square feet, they had to sublet some of their work out. The boat-building plant of Stearns and McKay Company of Marblehead, next to the Burgess plant, was contracted with and began building pontoons and other woodwork that was needed.

Employee Benefits

The Burgess management took good care of their employees, and efforts were made to secure a good eating place in town to service the eight hundred employees. The management searched all over town for a place to have a meal. What was desired was a large lunchroom that would be able to take care of all the employees once daily. Two enterprising young Marblehead boys got wind of this and came to the rescue on a small scale. One of the boys, Frank O'Keefe, age fourteen, of 16 Commercial Street, appeared at the gates of the Redstone Lane plant at noontime with appetizing dinners that he sold for twenty-five cents each, supplying twenty-five to thirty dinners, which vanished inside of ten minutes. Many workers were disappointed in not getting the hearty meal of boiled ham, boiled cabbage, two potatoes, bread and butter and a cup of coffee, all furnished by a Mrs. Welch. They brought the food in big baskets and served it on plates with knives and forks. So pleased was the Burgess Company with the service that a larger stand was provided outside the plant for them to serve their dinners. A local waterfront restaurant in town also welcomed the workers for lunch.

FEMALE WORKERS

Due to the number of men entering the service, the Burgess plant began hiring women. In the summer of 1918, it employed schoolteachers and high school students (my grandmother Emma Woodfin Foss Smith being one of them), who took the opportunity to do their part in helping to win the war and at the same time earn some extra money for their families. The hiring of the women started as an experiment, but they proved to be so efficient that they received increases of 25 percent in wages voluntarily given by the company. Some 150 women were employed, mostly working on the wing works, in which they were shown to have the greatest adaptability. Plant No. 2 employed even more women, and while their pay was not as great as the highest skilled men, it was well above what was paid to women in other industries. On some parts of the work the women proved themselves superior to the men. One foreman said, "These women only have to be shown once, as they use their heads," speaking of why the women excelled at their work.

Many of the women worked in the sewing department. Because of the great shortage of linen, which was being used elsewhere to make bandages for the hospitals, all the wings of the practice planes were made of mercerized cloth. This was applied to the wings on the bias, and the different pieces had to be sewn together. This work was done by double needle machines in the sewing department of the plant, where there were seventy-five women who turned out the cloth for six planes a day. They also made what were known as "sea anchors," which were made of heavy canvas, with the stitching done by the women while the men spliced the rope. Some women operated wire-stitching machines, using steel wire to unite the reinforced pieces. The women also worked in the disassembling department, where the planes that had been put together and inspected then had to be taken apart for shipping. The women greased all the wires and wrapped up all the separate parts. One task the women performed was far from easy and required a lot of strength: pulling the cloth over the wings. This work was done by hand, as the cloth was put on the bias and no mechanical means had been devised to perform this task. A team of sixteen women did all the safety wiring in the fuselage compartment, and on some of these tasks, they were quicker and better workers than the men.

END OF PRODUCTION

In October 1918, the Burgess Company held a parade for the kickoff of the Fourth Liberty Loan campaign. Aviators used the Burgess planes to fly over the town, dropping leaflets urging the citizens to purchase immediate subscriptions to the loan. The workmen and other employees of both plants took part in a parade throughout the town. There were many floats showing the construction of the battle planes.

In August 1918, the making of the airplanes for war use began slowing down, and the student and teacher workers returned to school. The aircraft program of the navy was well supplied by this time; however, the supply to the army was lagging behind. Shortly after 6:30 p.m. on November 7, 1918, the day of the false armistice, the Little Harbor plant burned to the ground. This was the third worst fire in the history of Marblehead. Thankfully, there were few workers in the plant, as they had suspended work in the early afternoon after hearing that the war had ended. A worker was in the engine room of the plant and heard a loud explosion and rushed outside to find the paint shop in flames. This was followed by several more explosions, and within minutes the entire building was engulfed in flames. The residents on Orne Street, fearing their homes would be lost, quickly got their valuables out of their houses. Furniture and valuables lined both sides of Orne Street. The damage to the plant was upward of $1 million, and all the company records were destroyed. The workers would use their personal tool kits

Burgess plant employees hold a parade, Orne Street, Marblehead. *Author's collection.*

at work, some being worth hundreds of dollars, and these were all lost in the fire. The plant was never rebuilt, and by March 1919, the making of airplanes had ceased operations at the Burgess plant at Redstone Lane. This was a real blow to Marbleheaders, leaving many people unemployed.

JOHN SIMMONS & COMPANY

Another business that prospered and gained work during wartime was John A. Simmons & Company, sailmakers located on State Street. They were awarded an army contract for the making of thirteen hundred army tents, with the delivery to be made in seven months' time. This project called for 140,000 yards of khaki-colored canvas furnished by the government, the first shipment arriving September 1, 1917. This contract came in the nick of time, as the sailmaking business was falling off due to the cessation of the yachting events in town. The company employed twenty-five people for this project, most from Marblehead. Mr. Simmons did have to purchase a new row of sewing machines, as well as having to get his loft faced up with beaverboard to make it warm enough for work during the winter months. He also found it necessary to add on more room in order to improve production, so he rented the room above the Bay State Fish Market on State Street. It was here that the workers cut the fabric and did some stitching. The output of tents was between fifty and one hundred per week.

By mid-September, Simmons's operation was in full swing, and the first shipment was sent out by the end of October. Unfortunately, the process did not go as smoothly as he had anticipated, as the material arrived slowly due to the lack of rail cars, which also delayed the delivery of the tents. The tents could not be sent until a government inspector came to town and signed off on them. The government then changed the color of the khaki, instead choosing to use a gray color, as army experts believed the color was more suitable for the time of year the tents would be used and gray blended in better with the landscape. This change caused a delay in obtaining the fabric and a temporary halt in production, but by April 1918, some thirteen hundred tents had been sent to the government and were used by the servicemen in France.

In February 1918, John A. Simmons, head of the company, passed away at his home on Mechanic Street from pneumonia at the age of thirty-three. The company continued with his father at the helm. He had already been associated with the company, so production was not interrupted.

Chapter 3

'HEADERS HELP AT HOME

RELIEF WORK

While the men of the town were preparing for war or actually on the battlefield, activities and lifestyle changes were going on in town. Even though the United States had not entered the war as of yet, emergency relief work began in Marblehead during the summer of 1915. It was published in the *Marblehead Messenger* that an opportunity would be given to all women in town who were interested in helping the wounded in what was then called the European War by making bandages and other hospital supplies. The work began under the auspices of the Women's Department of the National Civic Federation, later called the War Relief Committee, with Mrs. Robert S. Peabody, Mrs. William R. Castle Jr. (a summer resident) and Miss Edith C. Fabens as heads of the local committee.[13] The first meeting was held at the YMCA on Thursday, July 1, 1915, with weekly meetings thereafter. The Singer Sewing Machine Company made a donation of three sewing machines to be used by the Marblehead women. During the first week, nearly ninety women worked on making sponges, bandages, absorbent dressings, binders, slings and invalid and fracture pillows to send to hospitals overseas. Most of this first shipment of 7,155 dressings was sent to the Belgians, who were the first to require immediate assistance after the German invasion. In March 1916, the women of Marblehead received a letter from the office of the queen of Belgium saying how much she appreciated the work the women did:

LePanne, February 11, 1916
Office of the Secretary of the King and Queen
Madame President—

The Queen has received the articles for the ambulance which you sent in the name of your committee. Her majesty is very appreciative of the sympathy and generosity of your society and has directed me to send your members the expression of her deep gratitude. Please accept, Madame President, my distinguished greetings.

Orderly to the King,
Pheudhome

The War Relief Committee submitted an accounting of its first year's accomplishments from July 1, 1915, to July 7, 1916, and it had supplied a total of 51,760 articles. This included hospital supplies as well as knitted clothing. The committee also collected $1,433.52 in donations to be used for materials. The women received many letters of appreciation from the hospitals and some from the soldiers themselves thanking them for their hard work. One nurse wrote and told how she was caring for a young soldier who approached the nurse and asked for "another pair of good American socks."[14]

In 1917, the women of Marblehead Neck organized a chapter of the Special Aid Society. The group consisted of 115 women, with Mrs. Richard Pope appointed as chairwoman. There were eighty-four branches of this society in the entire country, with their headquarters being at 143 Berkeley Street in Boston. This organization later merged with the American Red Cross. The Marblehead women began working on knitting sweaters, scarves, socks and mittens with the hope being that no soldier leaving from Marblehead would be ill equipped.

In September 1917, the organization began the preparation of sending Christmas good cheer bags to the Marblehead men in the service. They started soliciting the town for various items: tobacco (Bull Durham being the preferred brand), pipes, paper, envelopes, pens and pencils, pocketknives, toothbrushes and paste, safety razors and shaving soap, folding drink cups, games, cards, clothing and other necessities the men may need from home. They were also making plans to send 1,800 pounds of candy, which Mrs. Pope began making at her home, Dockledge, on Marblehead Neck. Mr. Girdler Stacey, one of the confectionaries in town, also donated some of his famous candy for the men. All of their efforts paid off, and in November 1917, an army transport carrier left for France. Barring an attack by a German submarine, the boys were expected to receive their packages in time for Christmas.

Reverend O.W. Warmingham wrote a letter from the townsmen to be sent to the boys at Christmas. It was read at a Sunday evening Mass meeting at Abbot Hall:

Marblehead, Mass
Abbot Hall, November 18, 1917

Dear Sons of Marblehead

It is Sunday evening in the old town and "the end of a perfect day." The churches are closed and silent though the hour is but a little after seven. Abbot Hall, however, is fully alight and alive with people. Would you know the meaning of this gathering? Well, the citizens of your town have come together tonight to remember you.

Christmas will soon be upon us, and knowing that you will have to spend the day away from us, we have felt impelled through sheer pride and affection to write you this Christmas letter.

Greatly we regret your absence we cannot but remember with pride that you were among the first of our town to respond to the call and command of World Duty. We would feel ourselves condemned did we not do all in our power at home to back you men up who are away from home, upon the sea, and at the front. We are glad to be able to say to you that Marblehead is proving herself true in her loyalty. Not only has the second Liberty Loan been carried through to success but we are just now nearing the close of a nation-wide campaign in which thirty-five million dollars are to be raised for Y.M.C.A. war work. Knowing that this agency is best fitted to minister to you in your needs at the front, Marblehead is most gladly contributing her full share.

This old town, as you know, has played a noble part in the national crisis of the past. In this day of world-crisis it is proud to know that it is being represented by you. More of our men, doubtless, will be called out to join you. If they are, we know that there will be no shirking. Be assured that we remember you most affectionately, and are hoping and praying for a successful issue of the world conflict, and for your return. You will receive many tokens of goodwill and affection from individuals and societies in Marblehead, but this letter comes to represent the community's thoughts of you and for you.

May God bless and keep you, our sons, at this Christmas time, and buoy you up with thought that you are fighting for the very thing for which Christmas stands, "Peace on earth and goodwill among men."

Proudly and affectionately,
Your fellow townsmen of Marblehead.

The Marblehead women were often called upon to prepare special orders for the government, one being to make three hundred "anti-vermin shirts" for the men in combat. These were shirts made of a special material that when completed were washed in a chemical preparation that made them better for wearing and permitted them to be worn without a change for up to two weeks. The women were given six weeks to complete this request and were able to do so with no problem. In November 1917, a request was received from Captain Frank Converse at Camp Devens for 180 pairs of flannel pajamas for the artillery men, including twenty-one Marblehead men. Still busy with their knitting, the women decided to form a junior league for this project, and the younger girls of the town fulfilled this order.

RAISING FUNDS

There were many fundraising events taking place throughout the town during this time, and most were heartily endorsed by the citizens. Most, if not all, of the fraternal and patriotic organizations in town held events to raise money at one time or another. In order to sustain enthusiasm for the war efforts, patriotic mass meetings were held at Abbot Hall, where townsmen and religious figures would speak, schoolchildren would sing patriotic songs and the people could gather for comfort and support. By the fall of 1917, the drives and meetings had increased with such rapidity that the townsfolk hardly had time to take a breath between events. Hardly a week went by when some sort of demand was not made upon their generosity. Between relief drives, government drives for the sale of bonds and war savings stamps, the average family had little spare change left in their pockets.

Along with raising funds to be used for the troops abroad or the government, funds were also raised to help the families of soldiers living in Marblehead, resulting in the formation of the Public Safety Committee, headed by Mr. Joseph Martin. In April 1917, another mass meeting of the townspeople was called to raise money for the relief of these families. Mr. J.N. Osborne chaired the meeting and developed a means to raise money. The dependents of drafted troops, Massachusetts men in the army, navy and national guard, were eligible to receive aid from the state up to $40 a month, but Marblehead wanted to have funds set aside to provide above and beyond this amount. It was hoped that during this meeting $1,500 could be raised, but in fact, $2,500 was donated.[15]

The Special Aid Society, along with its knitting projects, also had the duty to raise money for its chapter. The society often held dances, luncheons and fairs to raise the money. One such affair that Mrs. Richard Pope headed up was the Easter Monday dance held in 1918 that netted $200 for the relief fund. It was touted as the social function of the season, and most of the town attended to show their support. From 9:00 p.m. until midnight, the floor of Abbot Hall was filled with beautifully dressed women and their escorts dancing to the Salem Cadet Band, directed by Mr. Jean M. Missaud. Miss Lena Martin and Mr. Fred Lyons were very entertaining with their demonstration of the foxtrot, a new dance originating in 1914. The stage was beautifully decorated with evergreen trees and Easter lilies, furnished by Captain Harry Dane of the Sorosis Military Farm in Marblehead. Refreshments were sold and served by nine Girl Scouts from town, the Misses Edith Martin, Margaret Smethurst, Grace Parker, Mary Powers, Alice Gray, Ruth Rogers, Elsie Thompson, Evelyn Sumner and Jennie Clothey, all clad in their Girl Scout uniforms.

APPRECIATION FOR THEIR EFFORTS

Every week in the local paper there were numerous letters published from soldiers thanking the townspeople for their efforts and their support of the men serving their country.[16]

"On Active Service" March 5, 1918
Dear Friends—

I have received your gifts and I am very thankful for what you have sent me. It is the first one received since I have been fighting. Of course you people back home know that we are doing our bit. Well, we have been fighting for one and a half months without a single days rest and, believe me; the boys are pretty tired out. I am running a machine gun for Battery F, and I have my hands full chasing away the Boche airplanes. Our regiment was honored for the good firing it did the other night when the Germans attacked us, but they didn't get far. I will close, dear friends, hoping to eat my next Christmas dinner in dear old Marblehead.

John Mullen

December 28, 1917

Please accept my thanks for the mighty fine blanket which you sent me on behalf of the old town of Marblehead. While some of the cities and towns of Massachusetts are sending their boys smokes that are only too soon consumed, gum that will eventually wear out, or candy and sweets that knock the lining out of a soldier, Marblehead sends blankets to keep them warm, but another evidence of her very practical turn of mind. As far as we over here are concerned nothing could have been more acceptable. And it is a corker. I had occasion to try it out last night in the trenches and more than once my mind wandered back to the little town and the committee of thoughtful men who remembered their adopted parson somewhere in France. Please convey to them and the town my heartfelt appreciation.

Lyman Rollins, chaplain, 101ˢᵗ U.S. Infantry[17]

THE AMERICAN RED CROSS

The American Red Cross, established by Clara Barton after the Civil War, was greatly expanded during World War I. On June 6, 1900, the organization was given a congressional charter that mandated that it fulfill the provisions of the Geneva Convention by rendering aid to the wounded during wars and providing communications between family members and members of the U.S. military. As the Red Cross was a nonprofit charitable organization, it received donations from the public, and many new local chapters were formed. Marblehead did its part to provide for the organization.

In December 1917, Marbleheaders once again proved their generosity and patriotism in the answer to the call of the American Red Cross. After only being in existence for three weeks, a donation party was set up in the YMCA on Monday evening, December 3, in which nearly 250 men, women and children of the town joined to try to reach the town's quota of 1,700 members. During the week of December 17–24, 1917 a large membership drive was held all across the country to secure as many members as possible, with a membership fee of one dollar. Charles A. Slee of Marblehead, with the assistance of other townsmen, worked on organizing the most thorough membership drive Marblehead had ever had. The committee adopted the slogan "A Red Cross Member in Every Home," not meaning that one member would be sufficient but that would be the minimum needed to reach their quota, using his unique method of completely organizing the town in units of about one hundred houses in close proximity, being in the command of a captain and then dividing these into groups of five. With a squad leader living in one of the houses, he was able to canvass the whole town in very short order. Putting the "over the top" slogan to good use, in one week 2,398 new members joined. Almost every home in town had a Red Cross Service Flag displayed in its window, and everyone was asked that the flags be illuminated on Christmas Eve.

Along with donating money and becoming a member of the Red Cross, there was also lots of work to be done for the organization, similar to the work done by the Special Aid Society and other organizations. During the first week of existence, the Marblehead chapter of the Red Cross sent six cases of surgical dressings to Peter Bent Brigham Hospital in Boston to be forwarded on to France. A second shipment was sent to the Red Cross

Supply Department of twenty hospital sheets, 180 handkerchiefs, forty-three pillows and the following knitted articles: twenty-one mufflers, sixteen sweaters, fifty-five pairs of socks, four trench caps, six helmets, fourteen pairs of hospital socks, seventy pairs of wristers, two afghans, forty-three face cloths, eighteen eye bandages and fifteen floor cloths. Marbleheaders being so good at their jobs, the National Red Cross asked the Marblehead chapter to knit fifty to one hundred sweaters and several other articles of clothing and to ready to have them shipped in one to two weeks' time. Naturally, the women obliged, and the task was completed. Along with knitting for the Red Cross, the women were also knitting for their own relatives fighting in the war.

At one point a young man, Corporal Fred Robinson, wrote home to his mother requesting "sweets not sweaters":

> *In your last letter you spoke about sending me sweaters, mittens, etc. Now, please, please don't do it. I now have more clothes than I know what to do with or than I have room for. What I want more than anything else, and the only things I want, for everything else is provided for us, is stuff to eat. I have asked about five times in various letters for you to send me some Hydrox and some Nabiscos. But no, your mind is set on mittens and sweaters, that I would be very sorry not to appreciate, but that necessity would require me to throw away when we move from here, which we expect to do very soon.*

He wrote that he appreciated the kisses from Girdler Stacey, "they were elegant and much more appreciated than a hundred sweaters or a million pairs of mittens. A muffler would be of use, however, although cookies and candy are far and inexpressibly more important."[18]

In May 1918, the National Red Cross once again had a drive to raise money, and once again Marblehead did its part to raise its quota. The Red Cross was looking to raise $100,000.00 across the country using the slogan "Give Until It Hurts You." They wanted to show the boys on the front line that those at home were doing their best to provide as much material comfort to them as possible. Once again, Mr. Charles A. Slee utilized his strategic house-to-house canvass. The fire alarm blew 5-5-5 at seven o'clock in the evening of the drive, signaling the teams to start their canvass. People

HOME MADE CANDIES

TRY OUR

Peanut Butter

Fresh Cream Caramels

Fudge Bars

Maple Walnut Cakes

New Cream Almonds

Molasses Caramel Kisses

ALL NEW FRESH GOODS

MADE DAILY

—AT—

STACEY'S, 11 PLEASANT ST., :: MARBLEHEAD ::

Advertisement for Girdler Stacey's homemade candies. *Courtesy of* Marblehead Messenger, *January 11, 1918. Author's collection.*

who had commitments for the evening were asked to remain at home until their house had been canvassed. Once again the old town came through, raising $7,563.85.[19]

Marblehead once again became festive when on June 8, 1918, a large carnival was held on the grounds of Abbot Hall under the auspices of the Red Cross and run by the pupils and teachers of the high school to raise more funds. It was an evening of great activity and great spectacle. The grounds were illuminated with colored lights, and booths were set up to sell cake, candy, ice cream, lemonade, tonic and grab bags. There was also a bazaar where fancy items were sold. Miss Annie Millett set up a fortunetelling booth, where she told eighty-one people their fortunes. Dancing was held in Abbot Hall from 3:00 to 5:30 p.m., with music provided by the Catholic Club Orchestra. Two special dances, the flag dance and the tarantella, were held on the lawn and performed by the high school students under the direction of Miss Lucille Webber.[20]

At seven o'clock, there was a short parade from Abbot Hall down Washington Street, where it encircled the town house and went back up Washington to Pleasant Street to School Street, back to Washington and returned to Abbot Hall. The parade was made up of a platoon of police officers, drum corps and the minstrel troop headed by Mr. E.P. Pigeon. A large Marblehead banner was carried by William Orne, the Red Cross flag by Clarence E. Chapman and a big Red Cross poster by Stanley Stevens. The high school girls, wearing Red Cross nurse uniforms, marched with their respective class banner and numerals. The seniors had a purple and gold banner and the juniors blue and gold, carried by Clarence Rodgers, with Mary Johnston and Minnie Patterson holding the streamers. The sophomore banner was carried by Gordon Humphrey, and the freshman flag was carried by Dan Peach. There were seven girls carrying a big sheet to which was sewn a Red Cross, into which the crowd along the parade route could toss money.

Once back at the hall, a minstrel show was given, and at 10:00 p.m. singing of "The Star-Spangled Banner" and other patriotic songs was led by Mr. Horace Broughton. The dancing continued until 11:30 p.m.

Even the young children in town got together and raised money for the Red Cross, with seven young girls performing their original play in the barn of Mr. Benjamin F. Martin Jr. on Pond Street. The Misses Emeline and Elizabeth Martin were the first to have the idea when they chose their original play, *The Sporting Women*, which was composed by the girls during the previous winter. The cast included, besides themselves, the Misses Cora, Bessie and Amelia Peach, Miss Lena Phillips and Miss Muriel Wilkins of Danvers. Mr. Fred Peach helped the girls with the stage and lights. Two performances were given, one in the afternoon for the children of town and one in the evening for the grown-ups, both well attended. Along with the proceeds from the play and the selling of cake and candy, the girls were able to donate seven dollars to the Red Cross.

LIBERTY BONDS AND WAR STAMPS

In 1917 and 1918, the United States government issued liberty bonds to raise money for its involvement in the war. Secretary of the Treasury William Gibbs McAdoo created an aggressive campaign to popularize the bonds.

The government used famous artists to make posters and used movie stars to host bond rallies. The campaign created great community efforts across the country to sell the bonds. A loan committee was set up in Marblehead with Everett Paine, chairman; John L. Litchman, secretary; and Arthur S. Adams, William E. Bowden, William A. Brown, Greely S. Curtis, William J. Goldthwait, James E. Gorman, Herbert Humphrey and Charles A. Slee as members. The National Grand Bank in town was involved in receiving subscriptions from the people for the Liberty Loans. The coupon bonds sold for $50 and multiples of this amount up to $1,000. The registered bonds sold for $100 to $100,000. All bonds were exempt from all local and income taxation. A plan was adopted whereby working people could purchase bonds through the National Grand Bank by paying $2 a week. Many of the town's fraternal organizations united together and purchased bonds in the name of their organization, requiring a small donation from each of their members.

Mr. Everett Paine, president of the National Grand Bank, said, "People should take hold and help out the government by subscribing for these bonds. While we cannot all go to war we can do this much. Money is very essential to the government in carrying on this war."[21]

Mr. W.C. Gregory, one of the town's druggists, was quoted as saying, "The proper thing for everybody to do is to buy all the bonds that they can as they are helping the government just so much. Lots of people can buy a $50 bond and thus show their interest, as this may be the only way in which they can display their patriotism."[22]

Sale of the Liberty Bonds was slow to catch on in town, and one member of the committee said, "I do not know what the matter with Marblehead is, but it seems to me they need the presence of a U-boat right off Marblehead to arouse them to the need of the hour, money that the government must have. This money is absolutely necessary and if the government does not get it the Germans are liable to come right over here and then the property of the people now hesitating would not be worth anything for years to come."[23]

One Marblehead boy of fourteen bought a fifty-dollar bond with his earnings, going into the bank and putting down two dollars and asking for the bond. The condition on which the bonds were issued was explained to him, and he was told that he needed to pay forty-eight more dollars until the bond would be his and was asked if he could pay this, to which he promptly explained, "I have a job worth two dollars a week to me, so I guess I can pay for the bond. And besides that is the only way I can help lick the Germans."[24]. When others in town heard this story, they were put to shame and began purchasing the bonds.

Three more Liberty Loan drives were held throughout the duration of the war, and each time Marbleheaders pushed the town "over the top." The second drive began in October 1917 with the sounding of the town fire alarm whistle at ten o'clock on a Monday morning. During this drive, anyone who subscribed for a loan was given a "Badge of Honor" button. The third drive was in April 1918, and during this drive, the pupils in the ninth grade at the Story School made a true sacrifice to help their country. They decided to give up buying individual class pins, which was a tradition of the class, and instead to use the money to purchase a Liberty Bond, which would be presented to the school.

When You Fight--Fight

FIGHT as these American soldiers fought in the streets of Fismes. "They covered themselves with glory," the papers say. Of course they did—they are Americans.

They met the finest of the enemy's troops in a terrific hand-to-hand struggle. They used their guns—their bayonets—their bare fists. Every American soldier went after his man desperately, fearlessly, persistently, with one great driving purpose—to whip that Prussian Guard, to silence its machine guns—to win!

It's a pretty good way to fight—this American way. It wins battles over there, it will win a splendid victory over here—if we *fight* when we fight—if we buy Liberty Bonds to our utmost.

When you fight—*fight!* When you buy—_buy!_

Lend the way they fight–Buy Bonds to your utmost

This Space Contributed to Winning the War by
National Grand Bank and C. A. Slee

Advertisement for Liberty Bonds. *Courtesy of* Marblehead Messenger, *June 28, 1918. Author's collection.*

Another tactic used to help sell bonds was to sound the fire whistle from Box 42, which caused a large crowd of people in the neighborhood to assemble on Atlantic Avenue. It was here that Chief Engineer John T. Adams acted as chief bond salesman, urging those in attendance to purchase bonds. Following this, the hook and ladder truck was sent around town, and bonds were sold everywhere a crowd was gathered. The final stunt was pulled off at the Warwick Theatre when Captain Roy F. Bergengrin of the U.S. Ordnance Department brought to town a number of German shells, cartridge belts and helmets. These were put up as prizes for those buying bonds, while other items were put up for auction. Mr. Herbert Humphrey and Mr. Greely S. Curtis were in a bidding war for first choice of two articles. Mr. Humphrey won with a bid of the purchase of a $1,500 bond. Mr. Curtis got second choice on a bid of $1,000. At the end of the evening, $6,000 worth of bonds had been sold.[25]

By going "over the top" in the third and fourth drives, the town had the honor of flying an honor flag at Monument Park. This was a red bordered flag with a white interior field with three vertical blue stripes that was flown by every town that met its quota in the drive.

THE SPIRIT OF 1918

BIG PRODUCTION WILL WIN THE WAR

YOU COMPLETED **13** SO FAR THIS WEEK

YOU COMPLETED **11** LAST WEEK

BEST WEEKS RECORD **13** DATE 3/30/18

Tally of Liberty Loans published weekly in local paper. *Courtesy of Marblehead Historical Commission, Abbot Hall, Marblehead, MA, object ID 1961-002-03202. www.marbleheadhistory.com.*

War Savings Stamps was another patriotic program used by the United States Treasury to help fund the war. It was principally aimed at school-age children. On March 11, 1918, the town's campaign manager, Charles A. Slee, announced a plan to raise money for the U.S. government by having a "Ladies First" campaign. His plan called for the women of the town to make the first canvass of the town to solicit personally all of the citizens to purchase War Savings Certificates or War Savings Stamps. Mrs. B.G. Melvin was appointed chairwoman of this Women's Committee, with John F. Williams as treasurer and Mr. L. Thomas Hopkins as secretary. The people were urged to buy Thrift Stamps for twenty-five cents each. These were pasted into a folder called a Thrift Card, and when filled, each card was worth four dollars. By presenting the completed card plus twelve cents, these could be exchanged for a five-dollar War Savings Stamp, which was then attached to folders known as War Savings Certificates. When twenty spaces were filled, each certificate was worth one hundred dollars.

SAVE MONEY AND YOU SAVE LIVES

:·: :·: :·: BUY :·: :·: :·:

W. S. S.
WAR SAVINGS STAMPS
ISSUED BY THE
UNITED STATES GOVERNMENT

MARCH 11 to 16

The Marblehead Drive Is On

WILL YOU START BY BUYING A 25c STAMP

Advertisement to purchase U.S. War Savings Stamps. *Courtesy of* Marblehead Messenger, *March 1, 1918. Author's collection.*

Marblehead women distributing Liberty Loan posters dressed in Red Cross uniforms. *Left to right*: Misses Joanna Martin, Mildred Chapman, Evelyn L. Roads, Mary S. Lyon, Margaret Keith and Marion Martin. *Courtesy of* Marblehead Messenger, *April 19, 1918. Author's collection.*

"Pledge Yourselves One and All to War Savings,"
Says the President

Thrift and War Savings Stamp Drive

on

FLAG DAY, JUNE 14th

SOLICITOR WILL CALL UPON YOU

"The man who buys Government securities transfers the purchasing power of his money to the United States Government until after the war, and to that same degree does not buy in competition with the Government."

Advertisement for War Stamp Drive on Flag Day 1918. *Courtesy of* Marblehead Messenger, *June 7, 1918. Author's collection.*

MONEY RAISED IN MARBLEHEAD FOR WAR PURPOSES AS REPORTED TO THE LIVE WIRE COMMITTEE

LIBERTY LOANS

First Loan	$186,000.00
Second Loan	$247,000.00
Third Loan, Quota $229,000	$318,000.00
Fourth Loan, Quota $485,000	$700,600.00
Total	$1,451,600.00
YMCA	$6,200.00
Red Cross	$19,000.00

PUBLIC SAFETY COMMITTEE

Subscription for Relief	$4,600.00
Town Appropriation	$6,000.00
Total	$10,600.00
Live Wire Committee	$2,100.00
Special Aid Society—Ladies	$3,745.29
Allied Catholic Societies	$1,000.00
War Savings Stamps	$50,000.00
United Drive	$12,000.00
Grand Total	$1,556,245.29

This does not include any special funds raised by fraternal organizations to aid their members in the service.

Chapter 4

WHEATLESS, MEATLESS, HEATLESS DAYS

During the years from 1914 to 1918, like other cities and towns in the country, Marblehead supported the war effort in what were known as Herbert Hoover's "meatless, wheatless, sweetless and heatless days," nicknamed "Hooverizing." Shortly after the country's entrance into the war, it became evident that a nationwide movement would be necessary to encourage food production and control the distribution and consumption of food. Food was needed to send to our Allies, our soldiers both home and overseas and for ourselves, all causing a food shortage in the United States. In the spring of 1918, the National Food Administration was created with local boards throughout the country and dictated what could be consumed on the food chain and what had to be omitted. The high prices of food and the food shortages caused many changes in people's dietary habits and lifestyles.

MARBLEHEAD'S GREAT BREAD FAMINE

Most people in town did their grocery shopping and errands on Saturday nights, buying food for their Sunday dinner. On one such night in April 1917, Marbleheaders experienced what the Germans had been experiencing for a while: the lack of bread in bakeshops. Two causes contributed to

ABOUT CRACKERS!

While our allotment of wheat flour for cracker-making has been used up for June, Monday begins a new month. We shall begin on that day supplying the grocers with our famous

Marblehead Crackers and Peerless Pilot

Plan to make your chowders during the early part of the month when our crackers are on the market.

-:- N. B. LINDSEY COMPANY. -:-

Advertisement for N.B. Lindsey Baking Company. *Courtesy of* Marblehead Messenger, *June 28, 1918. Author's collection.*

VICTORY BREAD

Our country's wheat supply is getting very small.

If we all co-operate with the Food Administration we shall not exhaust it before the next crop is harvested.

If we are greedy now it means a diet of corn cake and brown-bread very soon.

Help to conserve the wheat supply by buying Victory Bread.

WE MAKE IT!   DO YOU BUY IT?

N. B. LINDSEY CO.

Advertisement for N.B. Lindsey Baking Company Victory Bread. *Courtesy of* Marblehead Messenger, *June 28, 1918. Author's collection.*

this particular shortage: the arrival of the naval reserves on Marblehead Neck and the increased demand for bread to feed them, and the fact that the bakers were making fewer loaves so as not to waste supplies. With the increasing cost of flour, sugar and milk, they could ill afford to waste food. As it was, the bakers were forced to increase their prices and change the size of the loaves they made. The N.B. Lindsey Baking Company in town dispensed with baking small loaves and would only produce one size, selling for $0.12 a loaf. Another baker in town, F. Boardman, raised his price from $0.10 to $0.12 a loaf. At this time, flour was selling for $14.25 a barrel, wholesale, sugar was costing several cents more and there was also an increase in the cost of lard and milk.

Not long after this, in September 1917, "wheatless days" were implemented across the state by the food director of the county, Mr. Henry B. Endicott. People were now told what they could and could not eat. He requested that households observe two "wheatless days" each week in order to save on wheat flour. The local bakers revealed that Marbleheaders were stubborn in their ways and did not respond very well to this appeal to omit bread on Wednesdays and Thursdays, as the bakers saw no decrease in the demand for bread in their shops. As a result of this shortage, bakers began making what was known as "diet" or "graham" bread, later to become known as "war" or "victory" bread. The N.B. Lindsey Company was the first to introduce this bread made from the recipe put out by the Food Department, as it was considered the proper bread for the public during wartime. It was made in sixteen-ounce loaves that sold for ten cents, as set forth by the government. It was said to be highly nutritious and not all that objectionable in taste. The loaf was made from dough that contained not over two pounds of shortening, three quarts of skim milk and three pounds of sugar to one barrel of flour. The flour was a mix made in government mills, very white and of good quality.

In order to keep the bread at the low price of ten cents, it was necessary for the women to stop making their own bread at home, as the government felt it was part of the patriotism of the country to buy bakers' bread. Beginning in April 1918, every household in the country that had on hand thirty pounds or more of wheat flour had to report it to the Food Administration. Cards were distributed to every home and were required to be completed and returned by May 4, 1918. Anyone neglecting to do so, or who made a false statement, could have been prosecuted.

Meatless Days

In October 1917, the food director issued another request of the people, that being to observe another day of eating fish. Tuesday was the day selected. The reasoning was that the government had to supply large quantities of beef, pork and ham to the Allies and soldiers, as these could be more easily shipped than fish. Endicott said "that the people of Massachusetts are educated in the proper use of fish and this additional meatless day should not be a hardship for them." This bulletin was not only directed to every household but also to restaurants, social clubs and institutions. Endicott further pressured the people by saying, "Those who do not observe this extra fish day will be in the position of saying to themselves and to others that they have refused the chance which was given them to do their part toward helping with this war."

Marblehead, being a fishing town, was able to supply its families with enough fish to replace the meat in their diets. Recipes were posted in newspapers and pamphlets were distributed in grocery stores with recipes on how to change their diets. One recipe posted in the local papers was that of a boiled fish and potato dinner. I'm not sure if this is where the famous and delicious "corned fish dinner," a Marblehead tradition, originated or not. The recipe used by my family and other Marbleheaders is:

Peel potatoes and onions and boil in a large pot, when almost tender add haddock filets that have been corned. (To corn a fish means to cover with a coarse salt and let sit for several hours, a way of preserving meats and fish.) Cook until the vegetables are tender and the fish is flaky. In a separate pot boil whole red beets. Salt pork is cubed and cooked in the fry pan, making rashers.

When everything is cooked it is placed on a large platter and served. Each person takes the potatoes, onion, fish and beets and "smashes" it up on their plate, making quite a racket at the dinner table. This mixture is topped off with a small amount of fat from the salt pork and some "rashers" are added. It is now ready to consume.

One local fifteen-year-old boy did his part to help the town add an extra day of fish by starting his own fishing business. He was not old enough to serve his country as his brother Leonard did, but the younger son of Mr. and Mrs. Lot C. Peach found a way to help his county. Using his own dory, and unassisted, every morning before school he would row out to the channel of Marblehead Harbor and set his trawls. Then, after school, he would take his catch to the local fish dealers and earn about fourteen dollars a week. He was quoted as saying, "I am doing my bit to help increase the food supply in accordance with the Government's desire, I am investing most of the money I earn to thrift stamps."

The government provided cooking classes and classes on food preserving to the women in town on a weekly basis. Professor Thompson and Miss Gunderson of the Essex County Agricultural College and the Essex County Farm Bureau led these lectures and demonstrations at the high school. They were always well attended by the women. Around town at the provision dealers, leaflets were passed out with new recipes for the women. Some had the catchy titles of "A whole dinner in one dish," "Do you know cornmeal?" and the most popular, "Food will win the war; don't waste it."

The local Girl Scouts took it upon themselves to pledge to do their part for the war. At one Girl Scout meeting, the members signed the following pledge in order to save food for a soldier:

> *I will give up—Meat one day per week; wheat bread and cereals one meal per day; candy two days per week; sweet drinks one day per week.*
>
> *I will—double the use of vegetables at dinner, also double the use of fruit at lunch and supper; and will try to help on securing milk for children of the soldiers.*

SUGAR SHORTAGE

Candy at Christmas was and still is a tradition; however, in 1917, the children did not find many sweets in their Christmas stockings. A nationwide sugar shortage was taking place. A large truck loaded with sugar would arrive in town and be distributed to a number of grocers, but it was not enough to meet the demand. Sugar, while not rationed at this time, was sold in very small quantities so everyone would be able to have some on hand. One family found a way to circumvent the process by sending their four children, one after another, to the store where sugar was sold in two-pound lots per customer. This family got a large amount of sugar at the expense of others in the town. Also during this time the government set the price of sugar to be sold in retail stores at a price not to exceed eleven cents a pound.

In one store, there was a near riot due to the eagerness of people to get what little sugar had been delivered. So many patrons crowded the store that the doors had to be locked and people could enter as others exited. Getting sugar in other areas of New England was even more difficult, and some Marblehead families were sending small quantities via mail to friends and families.

Mr. Frank N. Osborne, a provisions dealer in Marblehead, went to great lengths to procure sugar for his loyal customers. On a cold day in February 1918, he took a long, cold train ride into Boston to secure his allotment of sugar. Once there, he had to find a way to get the sugar home, so he hired a large truck from the Loham Brothers, loaded it up and headed back to town. For some reason, so the story goes, he was unable to get past Revere, either on the shore boulevard or the marsh road, and was detoured through Cliftondale in Saugus. He finally made it back to his store and kept the sugar in his office, locking it up at night in his safe. This was a man dedicated to his patrons.

It was announced by the U.S. Food Administration that effective July 1,1918, sugar rationing would begin in order to prevent a serious scarcity of sugar. Many factors contributed to this decision, including the demand from France for more sugar due to the capture of a great part of the French beet sugar area by the enemy. There was a decrease in the amount received from Cuba, lack of shipping and the loss of millions of pounds by submarines sinking the cargo ships. A three-pound-per-capita limit was put into place and included brown, loaf and powdered sugar. As a result, many people began using condensed milk in their recipes as a sweetener, and this product began flying off the grocers' shelves.

In August 1918, the sugar situation was so strained that the grocers and local food administrator, Mr. Coates, worked together to stop what was known as "repeating." This referred to the practice of people buying sugar in town and then going to Salem, Boston or other local areas to purchase more sugar than they were entitled to under the rules of the Food Administration. This ban on sugar was lifted in December 1918, but there was still a shortage as the refineries were still behind in supplying sugar.

Coal Shortage

The winter of 1917–18 was a long and cold one. The severity of cold weather had not been seen in this area for quite some time, and to make matters worse, coal was in short supply. It was so cold during the last week of December and the first week of January that the harbor actually froze over. Even though Marblehead had the luxury of receiving coal by either barge or train, delivery was still a problem. The barges were being used as transport ships for the troops, and the trains had to also be available to move troops and supplies. In September 1917, the supply became so scarce that people were asked not to light their furnaces until November 1 of that year, as issued by the New England Coal Committee. This caused many homes to have frozen pipes and exploding heaters, causing even greater troubles.

Due to this shortage, the streetlights in Marblehead were shut off at midnight to conserve coal, as it was estimated that forty tons of coal could be conserved each month with this practice. The local Fuel Committee also set forth a change in business hours for the shopkeepers in town. Retail stores could be open from the hours of 9:00 a.m. to 6:00 p.m., except stores whose principal business was groceries, which could open at 7:00 a.m. but had the same closing hour. Variety stores, cigar stores and fruit stores could open at 7:00 a.m. and closed at 8:30 p.m. Barbershops and cobbler shops could open at 7:00 a.m. and close at 7:00 p.m. All stores could stay open two nights a week until 10:00 p.m. Stores that sold drugs and medical supplies could remain open after the closing set for other stores but could not engage in any other line of trade. The other stipulation was that the stores could not use electric lights exceeding a total of one hundred watts during the night hours. Billiard and poolrooms, lodges and clubs had to close at 10:00 p.m. Dances could not be held on Tuesday evenings. Any stores that had accounts with newspapers or news distribution could remain open for the sale of papers as usual but could not sell any other goods during this time. Any lights intended chiefly to illuminate the show windows could not be lighted at any time. Thankfully, this order lasted only a few months until March 1918, when it was cancelled.

Church services and meetings made up a large part of people's social activities during this time, but due to the coal shortage, many parishes had to find alternatives to using their sanctuaries for prayer due to the large amount of coal needed to heat them. The Old North Church held its Sunday services in the smaller chapel, which took less coal to heat. The Methodist church abandoned weeknight meetings so as not to have to heat or light any part of the church and used the smaller auditorium for Sunday services. Some parishes began "cottage prayer meetings," where parishioners would open their homes for prayer services and meetings.

Chapter 5

ALL AROUND THE TOWN

TOURISM

Marblehead was known as the yachting capital of the world; boat enthusiasts and tourists would come from all around to participate in and watch the races. But things changed dramatically during the summer of 1917. The two large yacht clubs on Marblehead Neck, the Corinthian and the Eastern, curtailed their races that summer. Many of the larger boats were given to the government for use in transport and patrolling of the waters. This,

Marblehead Town House. *Courtesy of Dan Dixey.*

compounded with the ban put on Sunday driving, made the harbor barren that year. Pleasure cruising was not discouraged but sponsored races were not held, although the clubs remained open for social gatherings.

LACK OF CELEBRATIONS

Prior to the war, Marbleheaders celebrated all the holidays in a grand fashion, having parades, dances, sporting events and other social gatherings; however, the war changed all this. Memorial Day celebrations had been a

Fourth of July celebration, circa 1916, Pond Street Association. *Author's collection.*

festive time for Marblehead's veterans, who called it the greatest day of the year; however, in 1917, it was a very solemn day. In prior years, an annual dinner had been catered by the Grand Army of the Republic for the veterans. But in 1917, due to the high prices of food, they could not feed the men on the forty dollars that was appropriated for the event. The price of the small flags used to place on gravestones of the war veterans also increased, so this activity was abandoned during the war years.

The Fourth of July had been in previous years a gala event with fireworks, parades, bonfires and neighborhood gatherings, but it was very subdued in 1917. The Pond Street Association was one neighborhood group that in previous years had lit up the town with its festivities. From Redd's Pond all the way down to Mugford Street would be lined with illuminated Japanese lanterns. An archway was erected with flowers and banners celebrating the Fourth. There were parades, games and plenty of food, with the festivities beginning at one minute past midnight on July 4 and continuing long into the evening. Fireworks and bonfires were held at Redd's Pond on the night of the Fourth, all in celebration of the independence of the United States. In contrast, in 1917, the only observance was the tradition of the bells ringing from Abbot Hall and the churches around town in the morning, at noon and at sunset.

War Gardens

War gardens or victory gardens were planted all across the country on private properties in order to reduce the pressure on the public food supplies due to the war. In addition to indirectly aiding the war effort, these gardens were also considered a civil morale booster, with the hopes that gardeners would feel empowered by their contribution of labor and rewarded by the gardens grown. The first year that war gardens were used in Marblehead was 1917. In a proclamation, President Wilson said to the Americans, "Everyone who creates or cultivates a garden helps the country. This is the time for America to correct the unpardonable fault of wastefulness and extravagance." In town, Mr. James C. Graves donated some of his land and raised 70½ bushels of potatoes, 2½ bushels of dry beans, 5½ bushels of green beans, 6,570 heads of cabbage, 21 pecks of beets, 2 bushels of carrots, 7 pecks of turnip, 2 pecks of parsnips, 400 pounds of squash, 100 heads of lettuce and 300 ears of corn.[26]

In 1918, there were three acres of land being cultivated by forty-four townsmen in order to raise more food for the town. The land was secured by the Special Committee of the Public Safety Committee of Marblehead, with Messrs. W.J. Goldthwait, N.C. Lyon and William A. Walker serving on the committee for the second year. The tracts of land were donated by James C. Graves on Atlantic Avenue; Miss Jennie Knowland on Devereux Street; Mr. Chester B. Freeto and Mr. Ernest S. Whorf on Locust Street; and the Goldthwait Trust on Orchard Street. Mr. James A. Neal of Clifton (a section of Marblehead) gave the gardeners 2,500 tomato plants. Of these, 1,500 were sold, with the proceeds donated to the Women's Food Conservation Committee, 500 were cultivated in the war gardens and the remainder was given to people of the town for their private gardens.

NAVAL RESERVES ARRIVE

In April 1917, Marblehead began hosting naval reserves who were stationed at the Eastern Yacht Club to receive instructions on submarine chasing. They arrived several at a time until about four hundred men were camped out on the Neck. The men were quartered on what was known as the berth deck underneath the piazza of the clubhouse of the yacht club. Marblehead contractor Thomas D. Snow was hired to put up hooks for hanging four hundred hammocks. Two Marblehead boys, Irving Gale and Ernest Gregory, both ensigns, learned their skills in the training camp. The reserves were there to get into condition for actual warfare, and their life at the camp was strenuous. They worked hard for the greater part of the day, with little time allowed for recreation. They learned such things as signaling, gunnery, navigation, seamanship and the use of small arms. Along with the military training, the men also had to keep the camp clean and perform mess work, messenger and orderly work. Many of the men were accustomed to indoor work and now had to adapt to the outdoor life but felt they would return to civilian life greatly improved physically and mentally. Marblehead Neck was transformed into an armed camp as sentries forbid the approach to the public; passes were required of all

Eastern Yacht Club, Marblehead Neck, used for training of naval reserves in 1918. *Courtesy of Library of Congress.*

residents and tradesmen who had business on the Neck. The town was asked to support the men, and the local bakers and provision dealers were asked to furnish supplies. The Special Aid Society was in charge of making the men comfortable during their training, and they willingly offered any supplies that the men may need. They also supplied table linens, dishes and silverware, as well as reading material and games for their leisure activities. The town also furnished the men with overcoats, woolen blankets and sweaters. The women sent the men many loaves of cakes, baked only as Marblehead housewives knew how to do.

It seems the government did not provide much in the way of supplies for this training camp; it was more interested in getting supplies to the men overseas. This was made evident when on Sunday, May 5, 1917, there was a huge rainstorm and a representative of the Special Aid Society visited the camp and noticed that the men on guard duty had no rainwear of any kind.

In short order, a call was put out to the townsfolk, and twenty-five sets of yellow oilskins were taken to the Neck. Reverend Thomas M. Mark of the Marblehead Universalist Church was the chaplain stationed at the camp. He told the women of the Special Aid Society that the men of the training camp were greatly indebted to them and to the people of Marblehead for their kind assistance during their stay. In the words of one of the men, "Gee, but Marblehead people are kind."[27]

Life was not all hard work and no play though, as on May 23, 1917, by permission of Lieutenant Commander J.O. Porter, the boys were allowed to entertain their female friends and families. On a beautiful Wednesday afternoon, 150 people from Marblehead and surrounding towns were present for a fun afternoon of dancing and entertainment furnished by the Reserves Orchestra in the dining room of the yacht club. This was the last

Naval reserves, Marblehead Neck. *Left to right*: Ernest Gregory, unknown, Irving Gale. *Courtesy of Marblehead Historical Commission, Abbot Hall, Marblehead, MA, object ID 2004-028-0250. www.marbleheadhistory. com.*

public gathering for a while, as the dreaded influenza epidemic of 1918 began raging across the country. Stringent rules were issued by the local board of health forbidding all public assemblages, which resulted in closing churches, theatres and schools.

This was not the first health scare the town endured, as one of the reserves staying on the Neck, Walter D. Kipp of Newport, Vermont, put a scare into the town when he was reported as having a case of the measles. He was immediately taken to Salem Hospital for treatment; however, it was feared the disease may spread to the entire encampment. The health officer of Marblehead, Agent Stone, was kept busy looking after the reserves and assuring that the camp was kept as sanitary as possible, not only for the men but also for the residents and visitors to the Neck. Thankfully, no other cases of measles were reported.

Marblehead YMCA

The YMCAs of the country played a large part in the war both in the United States and overseas to ensure that the military men were well supplied with necessities, as well as providing entertainment for the troops. All the naval reserves on Marblehead Neck were given free privileges and all the courtesies available at the YMCA building on Pleasant Street in Marblehead. This was highly appreciated by the men, as they were able to enjoy the showers, baths, gymnasium and game room. The general secretary of the Marblehead YMCA was Mr. Frank Broughton, who was honored to provide these services for the men.

YMCA buildings and representatives were found in every training camp in the country and also overseas at the front. Lieutenant Charles H. Evans wrote home from "somewhere in France" in November 1917 saying, "I am a long way from home, but I find a YMCA wherever I go waiting for me. It is one of the most wonderful things to me to run across an American YMCA. They are everywhere."

Corporal Arthur Graves sent a letter to Mr. Broughton and told of his experiences in France:[28]

Medals presented to Arthur Graves from the Town of Marblehead for service in World War I. *Courtesy of Maureen Graves Anderson.*

"Somewhere in France"
March 9, 1918

Dear Mr. B:

I'm now sitting in a roughly constructed bunk about 20 feet underground, and by the aid of my candle, provided it lasts long enough, I'll tell you a little of our life "over here."

To begin with, these caves or "dugouts" are supposed to be shell proof, but I'd hate to see a "Big Bertha" land directly on top. However they are pretty safe from the "75s."

About three weeks ago my company went to the front. The first night the Boches gave us a grand reception. For a full hour and a quarter their artillery played a box barrage on our lines. If you don't fully understand this, I'll explain. About 40 German batteries opened up at the same time. It was a pitch dark night but the light from the bursting shells made it almost as light as day. The shrapnel was as thick as hail.

The only reason I can give for coming out alive is that God must have been with us. Finally the barrage lifted. At the same instant a large raiding party attacked our line. Our artillery and machine guns showed the Huns that the Americans were on the alert. A good many of them were killed and we caught prisoners. Our casualties were very slight. After this the night was fairly quiet. That was the program for one night. It gives you an idea.

Now I am a little ways behind the first line. Y.M.C.A. canteens are dotted here and there in some old ruined houses. They furnish free writing paper and envelopes. They also carry sweets, and believe me, they are good. We go so long without candy that when we do see it, it seems like a regular Christmas to us. They certainly do wonderful work here, Mr. Broughton.

But how I would like to drop into the 'Head Y.M. just now to play a quiet game of pool. There are no shells to bother you there and I could leave my gas mask for ten minutes without flirting with death. Maybe those days will come again, B; let's hope so. This writing leaves me well and happy. I hope it finds you the same. Remember me to the crowd.

Yours truly,
Corporal Arthur Graves

Another letter of appreciation for both Marblehead candies and the YMCA was expressed by Mr. Charles B. Chapman:[29]

"U Guess Where"
March 22, 1918

Dear Friends:

Gee, but candy from God's country, especially Stacey's peanut butter kisses, taste indescribable over here, and furthermore when such candy comes from the real patriots of this war for Democracy, it makes one's appreciation indescribable. When the history of the present conflict is written, the thoughtful acts of the people at home in keeping the spirit of the men in France at its highest point, can never be overlooked. Your aid to the Red Triangle can never be repaid no matter what the outcome of this war.

Here is one reason why. Before the introduction of the Y.M.C.A. hut into our camp, the majority of the company sought amusement in the surrounding villages. Since the opening of the hut, the result of your aid, about one-thirtieth give up the program that the Red Triangle furnishes to go to the unclean villages for amusement. And if these men stopped to think of the good movies, the corker boxing bouts and the outdoor games, baseball, basketball and volleyball, why the French would soon go broke. And this is only one instance of what the folks at home are doing.

Very truly yours,
Charles B. Chapman

JUNIOR NATIONAL GUARD

Captain Allister Grant, commander of the Marblehead Home Guards, organized a group of young boys from Marblehead, ages nine to fourteen, to form the Junior National Guard of Grant's Army. They followed the same process as the National Guard, including having weekly inspections. Wooden guns were made for them, similar to the style of a Springfield rifle. One Saturday in May 1917, the boys and their commander, armed with their wooden guns and swords, set out for a hike in which they marched from downtown Marblehead to the Eastern Yacht Club on Marblehead Neck. Once there, they were inspected by General Rush, who was there inspecting the reserve unit, and he complimented them on their appearance, martial and public spirits. The reserves showed the boys around their quarters and their ship, which was truly enjoyed by the little ones. Evidently, word was not given to the mothers as to their boys' whereabouts. The youngsters had left home at 10:00 a.m. and did not return until 2:00 p.m., missing their noon meal and causing great anxiety for the mothers.

DECORATIONS AND SINGING

Around town, you could see that the people had great patriotism for their country and the servicemen. In the windows of many homes were displayed small red bordered flags with a white center and one or more blue stars indicating how many from the family were serving their country. Hopefully no gold stars appeared, as those represented a soldier lost in battle. In the windows of businesses around town could be seen brightly colored posters showing the success of whatever drive was taking place at the time.

On August 30, 1918, President Wilson requested everyone in America to sing "The Star-Spangled Banner" at 9:00 p.m., and of course Marbleheaders willingly participated with great fanfare. All over town, at the movie theatre, at whatever meeting was taking place, in the streets and in their homes you could hear the singing of the song. From 8:30 to 9:30 p.m., some fifteen hundred citizens gathered on the steps of the Old Town House, where the singing was led by Reverend Richard W. Boynton of Buffalo, New York, and Reverend O.W. Warmingham gave a speech on patriotism.

WARWICK THEATRE

During this time, movie houses were cropping up across the country. Marbleheaders had been watching minstrel shows and attending lectures in the Lyceum Hall located on Washington Street near the Old Town House since 1844. While the Warwick Theatre was being built on Pleasant Street in Marblehead in 1917, Mary Pickford was in town filming *The Pride of the Clan*. The Warwick officially opened on April 10, 1917, with Mr. E.B. Thomas of

WARWICK THEATRE

WEEK OF NOVEMBER 11, 1918.

MATINEES AT 4. SATURDAYS AT 2.30.　　　　EVENINGS AT 8.

MONDAY　Carlyle Blackwell in **"BY HOOK OR CROOK"** 6 Reel World **Wm. Duncan in "A Fight for Millions"**	**THURSDAY**　Viola Dana in **"THE ONLY ROAD"** 6 Reel Metro **"THE EAGLE'S EYE"**
TUESDAY　Live Wire Committee **"PERSHING'S CRUSADERS"** 7 Reel Government Film Mat. at 4.　10-15c　Evening, 7 & 9.　25c	**FRIDAY**　Norma Talmadge in **"DE LUXE ANNIE"** 6 Reel Select **"THE NATURE DANCE"**
WEDNESDAY　Gladys Leslie in **"THE SOAP GIRL"** **Charlie Chaplin in "ONE A.M."**	**SATURDAY**　Louis A. Stone in **"INSIDE THE LINES"** 6 Reel Special **"HANDS UP"**

Warwick Theatre advertisement during the week of the Armistice. *Courtesy of* Marblehead Messenger, *October 11, 1918. Author's collection.*

Cambridge the manager. John Morgan and Miss Gertrude Vincent were in the ticket office, and Knott H. Bartlett was the ticket taker and custodian. On opening night, the theatre was filled to capacity and several hundred people were outside waiting to get in. The stage was decorated with flowers and American flags, and a bugle was sounded to announce the grand opening. A brass quartet from the Okos Club in town was on hand and played "The Star-Spangled Banner," assisted with an accompaniment on the grand organ that was purchased for the theatre. All the proceeds from the evening's event were donated to assist the men of the Tenth Deck Division. A large picture of the Tenth Deck Division was auctioned off and won by Mr. Greely S. Curtis, who presented it to the Tenth Deck to display in their headquarters.

Chapter 6

MARBLEHEAD BOYS SERVE THEIR COUNTRY

IT'S YOUR DUTY

Prior to the U.S. involvement overseas, many Marblehead boys had already enlisted in the service and were serving their country by defending the Mexican border. The true realization of war did not occur until May 1917, when President Wilson ordered the enlistment of all able-bodied men who met the requirements for enlistment at that time. Notices were published in the Marblehead newspaper reminding the boys that the proper thing to do was to enlist in Marblehead so the town's mandated quota could be met. A recruitment committee was set up in town with Captain Charles A. Slee, Captain W.P. Nichols and Postmaster John F. Williams being appointed to the committee and Captain Slee offering the use of his office as the recruitment station.

Sunday, May 17, 1917, was set aside for another grand public patriotic demonstration to rally enthusiasm for the men who would be enlisting. The Home Guards committee invited all local societies to participate in the festivities. The committee consisted of William D. Wright, Joseph Martin, David Love, William J. Goldthwait and Representative John D. Osborne, chairmen of the selectmen. This parade was touted as the "biggest parade of its kind ever held in this town," with several thousand men marching, at least six marching bands and several drum corps, as well as representatives of all the local societies. The chief marshal, Colonel Frank A. Graves, with William Wright as the assistant marshal and Joseph Martin as the chief of staff, would lead the parade throughout the town, congregating at Seaside Park on Atlantic Avenue.

Once at the park, John J. Walsh and Daniel McKay, members of the Massachusetts Committee of Public Safety from Boston, would give the principal addresses. Local clergymen would offer prayers, and the schoolchildren would recite the Pledge of Allegiance and lead the crowd in "Marblehead Forever." Located around the park would be tables for recruiting men for the war and tables selling Liberty Bonds.

Everything was well planned; however, the weather did not cooperate, as around 11:00 a.m. heavy rains began, lasting until late in the afternoon and washing out all festivities. It was decided to abandon the parade. Word had to be sent out, but one thing not planned was a central parade headquarters where information could be disseminated. Although the parade was cancelled, a few hardy souls arrived ready to march, and a short parade of about four hundred marched to Abbot Hall, where the exercises began inside at 2:00 p.m. Some of the banners hanging in the auditorium gave the sentiments of the day, "The Price of Liberty Is Eternal Vigilance. Be Vigilant. Enlist or Buy a Liberty Bond, Here and Now," "State Guard Unit Is Sixty Men. Shall Marblehead Have a Unit? You Decide It Today" and "Training Will Do You Good. Enlist Here and Now."

The assessor's office in town supplied a report to Town Clerk W.R. Litchman to certify that there were 1,221 men between the ages of eighteen and forty-four years of age who were eligible for military duty in Marblehead in 1917. June 5, 1917, was the day set by President Wilson for all males who had reached their twenty-first birthday and not reached their thirty-first birthday to register for service. It was a one-day registration, distinct from the draft. Men were told it was their public duty and if they did not register they faced a penalty of imprisonment. Marblehead, Swampscott and Nahant were grouped together as one draft area, and the local Recruiting Committee sent the following letter to all eligible men.

Dear Sir:

You are one of the men available under the proposed draft for which you will register on Tuesday, June 5, 1917, read the following carefully.

Marblehead Boys Serve Their Country

There are 483 men in Marblehead between the ages of 21–31, liable for service under the recent draft act which you have read about in the papers. Estimating that 100 men between these ages are at present in some branch of the service, such as the Tenth Deck Division and Salem Companies, etc. there are 383 liable for service, of which approximately 50 per cent will be exempt because of dependents, physical disqualifications, etc., leaving 190 men who have no reason to be exempt. If the war lasts two years, which the President is preparing for, and all reliable authorities cannot see otherwise, the United States will call out less than 5,000,000 men which means that Marblehead's quota of 190 is practically certain of being drafted into the Army. Realize what that means—that every man drafted will see fighting.

Here is what we advise you to do. We have the authority from Commander Mitchell of the Navy, who is supreme in this district, that he will enroll as many men as we can get as a unit for Class 2 of the Naval Reserve Force, to be enrolled at Marblehead and to go from Marblehead.

Understand what this means. If the 190 men enroll in these units or divisions of 56 men each, similar to the Tenth Deck Division, they will be among friends and in a branch of the service very remote from being killed or wounded, and in a branch that Marblehead of all places is most suitably qualified to furnish men for, also they will always have a place to sleep and are reasonably sure of having the best to eat.

You have until Monday night to enroll, and as the time is short, a meeting will be held at Abbot Hall at 2:30 p.m., Sunday, June 3 when everything will be explained fully. If you are one of the 190 men, think carefully what this means to you and your future and do not have cause ever to regret that you did not enroll in the service, where your chance of being maimed for life is at a minimum, remembering that Marblehead will need you men in the trying times that are sure to come after the war and the experience that you get will more ably qualify your for these times.

Read this over until you can grasp the situation fully, as we request that all eligible men enroll before Monday night, and if the entire 190 men enroll Marblehead's quota will be taken for all men between these ages and you will always have the satisfaction of knowing that you volunteered and that Marblehead will have credit for sending her quota as volunteers.

For your own benefit be present Sunday afternoon at Abbot Hall.
Present this letter for admission to the Hall.

For your best interest,
Recruiting Committee
Charles A. Slee, Chairman
John F. Williams
Girdler Stacey

The scene at Abbot Hall on June 5, 1917, was very lively, with automobiles arriving and departing all day with the men who needed to register. The bell in Abbot Hall and the church bells around town were rung from 6:30 to 7:00 a.m., 12:00 to 12:30 p.m. and 7:00 to 7:30 p.m. to let people know that the registration was going on. Policemen guarded the entrance to the auditorium of Abbot Hall, and no one but those registering was allowed in. After registering, the men had to exit through the anteroom in the southeast corner, where they were given buttons marked "Enrolled for Service," attached to which was a piece of tricolored ribbon furnished by the board of trade of the town. Several young women—Priscilla Whalen, Edith Goodwin, Johanna Martin, Dorothy Peach, Martha Pouchain, May McHugh and Alice Eustis—were assigned to pin on the buttons. All were wearing white dresses with tricolored sashes. When it was over, 553 young men in Marblehead said, "We are ready Uncle Sam" by enrolling for service. All men who were supposed to register did so, with the figures being 38 aliens (those men not from Marblehead), 1 alien enemy (of German descent), 1 Negro and 533 Marbleheaders.[30]

RECEIVING ORDERS

In August 1917, Marblehead men first began receiving their draft notices, and each would receive a letter from the exemption board ordering him to appear for a physical examination by the doctor. He then went home and waited for further word telling him if he was a soldier or not. When he received the word, he was told to report the following day at 8:00 a.m., leaving little time to say his goodbyes to family and friends. Some of the men were assigned to the 101st Field Artillery and 104th Infantry, most being

Marblehead Boys Serve Their Country

National Guardsmen attached to the Salem Militia Company who reported to Camp Devens in Ayer, Massachusetts, for training. The first deployment of men from Marblehead was on September 20, 1917, when the boys made their way to Swampscott by trolley or train, thus marking their entry into the service. From Swampscott they went to Boston, and from there took a train to Ayer, Massachusetts. All they were allowed to take to camp with them were handkerchiefs, two pairs of white flannel pajamas, knitted socks to sleep in, a sleeveless sweater, three face towels, two bath towels, two dish towels, a laundry bag, a Boy Scout–type jackknife, a fountain pen, a shoe brush and tan paste, a razor, a shaving brush and soap, soap in a container, a toothbrush and paste, a wristwatch and a flashlight. None of these articles was furnished by the war department.

Naturally, Marblehead did not let the men leave without a great deal of fanfare. As the men did not leave all at the same time, there were many such sendoffs. On the day that men left, the businesses in town suspended their

Men off to war, 1918, Marblehead. *Courtesy of Marblehead Historical Commission, Abbot Hall, Marblehead, MA, object ID 1961-001-00651. www.marbleheadhistory.com.*

Parade for troops, Pleasant Street, Marblehead. *Courtesy of Marblehead Historical Commission, Abbot Hall, Marblehead, MA, object ID 1961-002-03346. www.marbleheadhistory.com.*

Parade for troops, Marblehead. *Courtesy of Marblehead Historical Commission, Abbot Hall, Marblehead, MA, object ID 1961-300-03302. www.marbleheadhistory.com.*

work after they heard the church bells ringing at 8:00 a.m., announcing the departure of the men. Friends and families lined the streets along the parade route from Abbot Hall to School Street to Essex Street and to the depot on Pleasant Street, all waving American flags, singing and wiping away their tears. The parade made a brief stop at Monument Park, where brief remarks were made by town officials and the schoolchildren led the crowd in singing "The Star-Spangled Banner," "America" and "Marblehead Forever." American flags were hung from homes and businesses and were attached to trucks, automobiles, bicycles and horses, showing a sea of red, white and blue all around town. Each man was dressed in his khaki uniform and carried over his shoulder the new woolen blanket given to him by the Public Safety Committee in Marblehead.

As the train pulled out of the station, there was a mass waving of handkerchiefs and lots of cheering, the platform packed as full as it could be. Each soldier was given a box lunch, paid for by the government, and a package containing cigarettes and snacks provided by the Public Safety Committee. The Special Aid Society presented the men with a knitted sweater, woolen stockings and a sewing kit; some were given knitted helmets and wristers. Those who did not receive all the equipment that day would get them as fast as they could be knit. The Marblehead delegation had to be the most well-equipped company at Camp Devens.

Ezekiel Russell Peach in World War I uniform. *Courtesy of Zeke R. Peach Jr.*

Five lads off to war in 1918 in front of the Warwick Theatre, Marblehead. *Front row*: Daniel H. Colbert and Clarence R. Chapman. *Second row*: Morrill S. Reynolds, Arthur Cooksey and Wilbur Merrill. *Courtesy of* Marblehead Messenger. *Author's collection.*

Men off to war standing on the steps of the town house, Marblehead. *Back row, center*: Stewart Smith. *Courtesy of Barbara Taylor.*

Day inducted into the army, May 31, 1918, in front of Warwick Theatre, Marblehead. *Front row*: Hump Winslow, Carl Stone, Joe Stacey, Walter Blackler, Pah Parry and Bill Farry. *Back row*: Stewart Smith, Frank Kidder, Zeke Peach, Joe Caswell, Mish Robbins, unknown and Giant Perkins. *Courtesy of Zeke R. Peach Jr.*

LIFE AT CAMP DEVENS

Camp Devens was one of thirty-three National Guard containments in the United States. Many of the men suffered from homesickness when they first arrived. For many, it was their first time away from family and friends.

An article in the *Marblehead Messenger* on November 23, 1917, was written to tell the townsfolk what life was like for the men at the camp, told from the writer's observation upon visiting the men. The brown clad battalions would begin marching over the dead grass fields for two miles to begin their drills at 7:30 a.m. Other battalions could be seen shouldering picks and shovels, winding up over the hills to dig trenches. Captain Charles E. Salek, a New York physical education director, would put the men through forty-three minutes of army gymnastics to prepare them for what was to come. A regiment of artillery, the 301st Light Infantry, was in the fields practicing pitching pup tents, while another regiment of artillery could be seen drilling in platoon groups with its wooden field pieces. The carpenters

Camp Devens. *Courtesy of Fort Devens Museum.*

Camp Devens. *Courtesy of Fort Devens Museum.*

of the regiment were rushing arsenal work by putting together old wagon wheels gathered from the many farms of central Massachusetts.

At noon, the men were given a half hour of "spare time," during which they could be seen sitting on barrack steps reading newspapers or in the barrack yards playing football. The men resumed their drills until 4:00 p.m., when they would get ready for supper, which was at 5:15 p.m. At 6:00 p.m., the camp was ready for a long evening of revelry. In the evening, some of the men would crowd the sidewalks of Ayer or take the train to nearby Fitchburg. Inside the camp there were ten YMCA buildings, two Knights of Columbus buildings, one theatre and nine post exchanges where the men could enjoy some free time. They could also attend classes in French, English and other studies. Checkers was the game of choice in the camp. The men also made their own entertainment by singing, forming bands and putting on talent shows. At 10:00 p.m., the regimental bugler would play Taps, and all was quiet.

Word was received from Camp Devens that the men would like to receive magazines and newspapers from home, so the YMCA set out to fulfill their request. The following letter was received in response to their generous donation:[31]

Battery B 301st Field Artillery
September 24, 1917

Dear Madam:
We received today by way of American Express Co. a box of magazines for the use of our battery. We are more than delighted with them, as it is just what the men need very much for their hours off from duty. It is already evident that the Marblehead people are doing a great deal for their men that are in the service. Their sweaters are excellent and in these last few days have been very necessary.
We appreciate this kindness and thank you very much.

Very sincerely yours,
Frank L. Converse
Captain, 301st Field Artillery

In November 1917, Chief Engineer John T. Adams of Marblehead made a visit to Camp Devens and brought with him lobsters, potato chips and other fixings for the local boys in Company B. Forty-eight generous citizens of Marblehead contributed to this down-home meal. Two automobiles were used to transport the party of Adams, Gardner R. Hathaway, S. Frank Chapman, Clinton Foss (my great-grandfather), George Harris, John F. Brown and Clinton Adams. No time was lost in cooking up the feast, and the familiar odor of boiling lobster was present throughout the camp. Captain Frank Converse, commander of the post, was a welcome guest of the men. The 130 pounds of lobster were shared by the Marblehead boys with their messmates, numbering 190 men each enjoying a tidbit of the delicacy.

As much as the soldiers would like to be home with their loved ones, they knew it was their duty to serve their country. Mr. and Mrs. George S. Pierce of 55 Commercial Street, Marblehead, received the following letter from their son Alden, serving in a training camp in February 1918.[32] Alden was born November 7, 1893,[33] and was a farmer and gardener for Mr. H.L. Bowden of Marblehead Neck. He married Elsa L. Nyberg on April 12, 1917, just prior to joining the service in June.[34]

> *Dear Mother and Father:*
>
> *I received your kind box that you sent me and I also received the blessed cross which I have now around my neck. I am thankful to you both and Aunt Molly also for the nice box you sent. I forgot to tell you three weeks ago when I wrote, that I went to confession and made my Christmas duty.*
>
> *Mother, don't be too sure about me coming home on a discharge. I can get my discharge if I wish to complain, but I have thought the matter over seriously and I feel that I would rather stay in the service and do my duty the same as millions more. I know you would like to see me home, and I would love to be home myself with you all, but I will feel much better if I stay and fight with my pals.*
>
> *Every fellow in here has someone dear at home as well as I have and they, too, would like to be home as well as I, but today it is the duty of every young fellow to be at war in this country and help win the war for your protection and everyone dear at home.*
>
> *I know you would feel better if I was home, but now is the time to forget home until we have won. You would feel much better in the end if I did my duty. I know you would, like millions of mothers who have their sons in here...*

I hope to get a furlough soon, but if I shouldn't, just cheer up until I get home again. I will close at these lines, sending my best love to you and father, and all my friends till we meet again.

From your loving son,
Alden

TRIP ACROSS THE OCEAN

The men who were training at Camp Devens were able to return home several times on furloughs and could say their goodbyes before crossing the ocean. While the Red Cross sent postcards to family members telling of the safe arrival of their soldiers, they were very brief and to the point: "Your son has arrived safely." People back home learned about the life of the soldiers by reading the letters that were sent home. One such letter from Alden Bartlett was received and read by Reverend Leslie C. Greely at the Old North Church's Men's Club meeting in November 1917.[35] Alden was the son of Woodfin and Cora Tucker Bartlett, born October 21, 1894, in Marblehead. He served with Company A of the Fourteenth Engineers and was injured several times during his tour of duty. He was hit above the eye from a rail falling off a car, causing a large gash over his eye. He also was sent to a New York hospital to recuperate from the effects of being gassed. He married Lydia Thompson Thorner on May 21, 1921.[36] The following excerpts are from his letter:

"Somewhere in France"
November 2, 1917

Mr. Dear Mr. Greely:
   I received several letters from home today and as usual they all came in a bunch. One of them told me that you would like to hear from me for the men's club, so I'll try to tell you what I can of our trip to France and as much of our work as I am allowed. We left Camp Rockingham[37] on July 28 for our port of embarkation. I'll never forget that last ride in real equipment over real railroads. We had the finest cars and only one man to a seat. I was on train guard (on this train) which enabled me to be on

SOLDIERS' MAIL.

THE AMERICAN RED CROSS

MILITARY
POST OFFICE

NO POSTAGE
NECESSARY.

THIS SIDE FOR ADDRESS ONLY.

Mrs Charles H. Smith
24 Beacon St
Marblehead Mass

THE SHIP ON WHICH I SAILED HAS ARRIVED
SAFELY OVERSEAS.

Name *Stewart Smith*

Organization

American Expeditionary Forces.

aug 14

Red Cross postcard sent to families when servicemen were safely across the ocean. *Author's collection.*

the platform and to observe the country through which we were passing. We spent the night on the train and the next morning we were transferred by transport to the boat on which we were to make our trip. She is one of the largest lines in the transatlantic service, but we, being only soldiers were stacked two deep, four to a room. The ventilation was not the best so Hal Day and I moved our mattresses and blankets to the deck, our bed for the voyage.

The next day we were to sail and that morning our Colonel granted liberty until 1 P.M. so we could stock up on tobacco and other things that we needed in New York at the Red Cross headquarters. We were given a bag and "fell in" as we went through the door and walked around the room holding our bags open. We received tobacco, playing cards, pipes, shaving soap, tooth powder and every possible thing that goes to make life worthwhile for a soldier. There were sweaters and gloves, stockings and helmets for those who were not so lucky as I was, by being provided with these things by our Special Aid Society.

From there we went back to the boat and at 3 o'clock we swung out into the stream. It seemed as if all the boats in the harbor had "cut loose" with their whistles. Everything from an incoming liner to a fisherman in a motor dory, gave us the three whistles of salute as we streamed down the harbor past the Statue of Liberty, the gift of the country for which we were destined.

The first days of the trip were uneventful except for the sightings of a few whales. On the fifth day out we ran into a storm and I was unfortunate enough to have a bad attack of "mal de mar." At first I was afraid the boat would sink and later I was afraid it wouldn't. This continued all the next day, when I was posted on "submarine watch" on the sun deck. I was so sick that I couldn't have seen a submarine if it came right up in front of us and on my second trick I had to be relieved. The seventeenth day we sighted a lighthouse and the next morning we were safely in harbor.

We disembarked at 3 P.M. on August 14 and were carried to our camp in England in those funny little English coaches that you have heard described much better than I can tell you. We rode in third class and it wasn't so very bad, at that. The trip across England was very interesting, so much so that we took turns riding at the windows so we could see the country. We reached our camp at 2 in the morning and were greeted by the "Star Spangled Banner." While we were unloading we heard a voice shouting, "Anybody here from Salem, Mass?", ten voices let out ten war-whoops at the same time with, "right here." The voice was of the Camp Secretary of the YMCA whose name is Trumbull and comes from Salem. We succeeded in getting into our tents for the first sleep on something solid for nearly three weeks.

We were out of luck on the mess question at this camp, but nobody died of starvation. On the third day we were told that we were going to parade in London and we were busy the rest of the day cleaning up. Shoe polish and whisk brooms were dug from the bottoms of our knapsacks and everybody turned to so we could look our best. We entrained the next morning very early and had another very pleasant ride through England to London. We marched from Waterloo Station by the House of Parliament to Wellington Barracks, where breakfast was served. We had bacon and eggs and tea, the first real feed since our arrival and with something substantial under our belts, we could have marched straight to Berlin.

The parade started at 11 in the morning from Wellington Barracks. From there we went over the route through Trafalgar Square up Piccadilly. We were reviewed by our Ambassador and Admiral Simms and at Buckingham Palace we were reviewed by His Majesty the King and the Queen and General French. From there we went to Green Park where luncheon was served. From there we went back to the barracks and entrained for camp again. The things that impressed me most were the crowds that turned out. The people were packed solid from the sidewalks to a space just wide enough for us to march through and it was one continuous cheer from the time we started until we left at Waterloo again. The Stars and Stripes were in evidence along the line and they flew beside the Union Jack over Parliament, and the Prime Minister adjourned a meeting of council to see us pass by. We were the first foreign troops under arms to parade in London since the taking of the city by William of Orange.

Two days later we left for France and our first few days in France were like the first few in England. We landed in a seaport town and had a fine chance to look the city over. We were all broke by this time and I believe the French were sadly disappointed with the "spendthrift American." I had nine sacks of Bull Durham cached in the pockets of my cartridge belt, so I was pretty well fixed for a while.

We were eight days in this camp while a detachment went ahead to prepare a place for us. While here they presented us with a steel derby, gas mask and smoke helmet. They taught us how to use them. Then they loaded us into freight cars labeled "quarente homes ou huit chevaux en longue," so you can see that forty men and equipment in cars that will hold eight horses lengthwise, don't have much room. They turned us out in the early evening *and while we were unloading we heard our first real noise of war. Air planes were up and observation balloons were in the air. In the distance we could hear the rumble of artillery. But that night it would have taken more than guns to keep us awake.*

This letter is written by the light of a candle on a table taken from a "Germ Hun" dugout and as the light is burning low, I must close. Please remember me to all.

Yours truly,
Alden T. Bartlett

TRENCH LIFE

Life in the trenches was a cold, miserable experience, and Leonard Oliver Peach related some of his experiences while serving as a member of Battery D, 101st Field Artillery, writing home about having a "cootie bath." He was the son of Lot Conant Peach and Arabella Jeffrey Peach. He was born in Marblehead on January 9, 1895,[38] and died July 8, 1976.[39]

On Active Service
September 29, 1918

My Dear Mother:

Sunday morning and plenty of rain. I have just come up from taking care of the horses and the mud is quite deep. I found a pair of German leather boots the other day and they are the only things that kept my feet dry. I look funny walking around with them on, but as long as they keep my feet dry I am going to wear them.

For all the hard times we go through there are some that make us laugh, although it means life or death to some of the boys. What I am going to tell you about happened yesterday. We were all due for a cootie bath and clean clothes. I got mine in the morning but some of the boys went down in the afternoon.

They were just having the water running on them when the Huns dropped a shell right in the cootie bath. No one was hurt, but they got a shower of mud, and the way the fellows ran over the hill without any clothes on would make one laugh and it was a cold day, too. We have been over here so long now we do not wait to see where the next shell is going to land as we used to do.

Your letter found me in good health, but many miles away from the hospital. My sickness was caused mostly from dead horses and men that had lain around in the sun too long. I can imagine what Ben told you when he was home, and you can put it down as the truth. I wished that I had known that he was in Bordeaux, as I think I was there the same time. I have not been paid in three months, but I don't need the money as they don't bring hardly anything way up here to sell so I have nothing to worry over.

That war garden of father's must have been some big by the letter you sent me telling that he had so many potatoes and other things. Those papers you sent have not reached me as I think they were sent to the hospital and are still following me around France. I have received some Sunday papers and there was a fine story in the American.

I guess we will never get rid of the cooties as long as we are in this country as we had some new clothes and they had them in. I wonder if they are going to keep us on the front all winter. If they do I hope the war will be over next week as one winter here was enough.

Lots of love to all,
Your son.
Leonard

Alfred R. Smith who served in Battery D, 101ˢᵗ Field Artillery, wrote a poem describing his life in the trenches of France, published in the *Marblehead Messenger* in September 1918.[40]

This is the song of the blooming trench,
　It's sung by us and sung by the French
It's probably sung by the German Huns,
　And it isn't all beer, biscuits and buns.
It's a song of water, mud and slime
　And keeping your eyes skinned all the time.
The dead Boches may kick up a stench,
　Remember that you have got to stick to your trench;
Yes, boy, stick like glue to your trench.

You dig when it is dark and you work when it is light,
*   And then there's the "listening post" at night.*
Though you're soaked to the skin and chilled to the bone,
*   Though your hands are like ice and your feet like stone,*
Though your watch is long and your rest is brief,
*   And you pray like hell for the next relief,*
Though the wind may howl and the rain my drench,
*   Remember buddie, just stick to your trench,*
Yes, stick like glue to your trench.

Perhaps a bullet may find its mark,
*   And then there's a funeral after dark,*
And you say as you lay him beneath the sod,
*   A sportsman's soul had gone to his God.*
Behind the trench in the open ground,
*   There's a little cross on a little mound,*
And if your heart strings feel a wrench,
*   Remember, he died for his blooming trench,*

There's a rush and a dash, and they're at your wire,
*   And you open the hell of a rapid fire;*
The Maxims rattle and the rifles flash,
*   And the bombs explode with a sickening crash.*
You give them lead and you give them steel,
*   Till at last they waver and turn and reel.*

You've done your job—there was never a blench,
*   You've given them hell, and you've saved your trench;*
By God, boy, you're stuck to your trench!!

LIFE ON A DESTROYER

Not all the boys served on land; many were on the high seas. Ensign Horton Brown was aboard a U.S. destroyer in Europe in which he was engaged in combating U-boats. Horton was the son of Henry Ware and Lizzie Graves

Brown, born on June 21, 1895.[41] He died on September 15, 1972.[42] He was one of the forty New England men selected to train at the Naval Academy at Annapolis. He wrote this letter to his sister, Miss Ella Brown:[43]

June 12, 1918

Dear Ella:

Wish to thank you ever so much for the book you gave me. It was very good indeed. Thank mother for the candy, all the officers enjoyed it very much. Am in the best of health and have a very agreeable bunch of brother officers. Last Saturday I went with the Captain to a dance and had a great time. The girls are very good dancers and entertainers.

Was out in a storm last trip and you can take it from me that this ship does pitch and roll. I have never experienced anything like it before and do not believe any other type of craft has anything near the same motion. We roll and pitch, shipping green seas of solid water across the decks and coming up onto the bridge. I got soaking wet and it seemed like the old racing days to be dodging the seas. Sleep was impossible, eating nearly as bad, two crackers for breakfast and two sandwiches for lunch. It lasted all night and the next day until we made port and believe me port looked good; although I was not seasick I was tired from trying to hold myself on a bunk or stand on my feet, holding on all the time with both hands.

The life is a rough and ready one as I have said before; we all sleep at sea with our clothes on, a life preserver for a pillow, and ready to go into action at a moment's notice. They issue sea boots, heavy underwear, socks and coats lined with sheepskin, so as to keep us warm. I will not know warm weather this year for at sea here it is always cold and very apt to be foggy, which does not help navigation.

Besides torpedoes I am assistant engineer officer and the captain expects to make me chief engineer in about a month when the chief we have now is due for a transfer.

While at sea we are kept very busy and hardly a day passes without some excitement and perhaps a little firing, but the destroyer with their speed and depth charges have the advantage, but not such a large advantage as to take all the fun out of the chase, for it really is a chase, for the destroyers are chasing the sub and the subs are taking all the care possible to stay out of their way for they are afraid of the American boats, but by this I do not want you to think that there are not a good many of them operating, for there are.

I have in this short while accumulated some very interesting stories and experiences of things that never appear in print and probably never will until after the war when the truth becomes known about what the American destroyers really have done, and believe me it will open the eyes of the American people and make them feel proud of their navy and realize what a high standard it has compared with the navies of the other countries.

Must close now with love to all,

Horton

FIRING THE FIRST SHOT

On Tuesday, February 5, 1918, at 3:45 p.m., the first shot by the National Guard was fired at the Huns by Section One of Battery A, 101st Regiment of Field Artillery. This regiment was part of the 26th Division, better known as the "New England" or "Yankee Division," a shock division of the U.S. Army in France. Many of the boys from Marblehead were assigned to this division. One Marbleheader, Edwin T. Martin, who enlisted on May 7, 1917, put the first loaded shell into the gun that was fired at the Huns. The shell that contained this shot is now at the State House in Boston. It was presented to the governor by Mrs. Sherburne, wife of Colonel Sherburne. It bears the following inscription: "To His Excellency Governor Samuel Walker McCall: The first shell fired by the National Guard against Germany by the First Section, Battery A, 101st Field

Edwin Thomas Martin, Battery A, 101st Field Artillery, Marblehead. *Photo from Live Wire Committee publication, circa 1919.*

Shell casing from the first shell fired by the National Guard, 101st Regiment, Field Artillery First Section, Battery A against Germany, February 5, 1918. *Courtesy of the Commonwealth of Massachusetts, photo by Bruce Diloreto.*

Artillery, Colonel John H. Sherburne Commanding, Tuesday, February 5, 3:45 P.M., 1918."

Edwin was born in Marblehead on August 21, 1896,[44] and died September 19, 1983, in California.[45] He was injured several times during his time at the front, the first being at Seicheprey, France, Toul Sector on April 21, 1918;[46] again at Chateau Thierry during the second Battle of the Marne on July 19, 1918;[47] and at St. Miheil Sector on September 24, 1918.[48] He was cited for gallant conduct and devotion to duty in the field on April 21, 1918, by Major General C.R. Edwards for his aiding of the wounded under hostile shell fire.

MARBLEHEAD'S CHAPLAINS

Four spiritual leaders from the Marblehead churches also served their country both in the United States and at the front line. The pastor of the Universalist church, the Reverend Thomas M. Mark, was assigned chaplain at Base Six, Brooklyn, New York, and the Reverend John F. Monahan, assistant rector of the Star of the Sea Church, was named chaplain of the Medical Corps at Fort Oglethorpe, Georgia. The Reverend Phanuel B. Covell, pastor of the First Baptist Church, was appointed chaplain of the Second Battalion Trench Motor, France, while the Reverend Lyman Rollins of St. Michaels Church was appointed chaplain for the Fifth Regiment, Massachusetts Volunteer Militia.[49] As soon as the call for troops was issued, Reverend Rollins was in touch with the military authorities

Chaplains from Marblehead serving in World War I.
Photo from Live Wire Committee publication, circa 1919.

saying that he desired to serve as chaplain. The first regiment he was attached to was based in Texas to patrol the Mexican borders. He later went on to serve in France.

Chaplain Rollins, the "Fighting Chaplain," told of his adventures in a letter he wrote to the town: "I have just come back from the front line—to rest up, clean up and fill up. During this battle I have not had my clothes off for weeks, but I must do so occasionally as I have to keep from getting cooties, if I can. We must even sleep with our boots on and a gas mask either around our necks or at our head." Chaplain Rollins's role was to baptize everyone in his regiment who requested it, no matter how intense the fighting was. He also attempted to administer Communion to all of the three hundred men associated with his regiment. For all his service and courageous acts he received two medals of honor, the Croix de Guerre from the French government for bravery displayed in May 1918 and the other for the Battle of St. Mihiel. During the fight for Argonne Forest on October 17, 1918, he was wounded and gassed because he had gone "over the top" to aid the soldiers rather than remaining below in the trenches.[50]

Edward Evans, who was serving in the 101st Field Artillery in France, wrote home and told his mother about meeting Chaplain Rollins and attending one of his services:[51]

"Somewhere in France"
Sunday May 2, 1918

Dear Mother:
   Just a line to let you know that your boy is thinking of you although I am not able to go to church all dolled up with a pink carnation in my buttonhole. Nevertheless, I will have to admit that did go last Sunday, and if you please, listened to a sermon by the Pastor of a Marblehead church. To be more plain, I found out that Rev. Lyman Rollins was going to be at M—a town about two kilometers from the battery position we were in at that time, so I asked my officer if I could have the morning off.
   After I got his permission I hurried down to the town and got to church just in time. As Mr. Rollins said after the service, when I was talking with him, he believed it was one of the most unique services he had ever held. It was held in the Salvation Army dugout, about fifteen feet underground.

The water was up to our ankles and the place was lighted with candles. The place itself was a solid concrete vault under the ruins of an old house.

About the middle of a song the Huns came in with a roaring brasso produndo in the form of heavy shells dropped directly on the roof and in the doorway of the dugout, but even that could not bother the Chaplain, so the service went right on.

Mr. Rollins still has the same old punch and go in him and he surely does get after the boys, but they all like him for it. I had quite a talk with the chaplain in his room after the sermon; he told me of some of his adventures in the front line. He showed me his hands, which were all covered with blisters. I asked him how he got the blisters and he very modestly told me, "Oh, digging graves." That is the worst part of the infantry they are always digging at something when they are not fighting.

Well, dear, remember I am thinking of you almost as much as you are of me and don't think for a minute that I wouldn't rather be at home than over here, but we will have to do as the French do, just smile and say, "C'est la guerre," or "it is the war."

Yours with love,
Edward Evans

Hundreds of Marbleheaders gathered at the entrance to Abbot Hall in early July 1918 in order to honor Reverend Rollins, who had recently returned from France. A parade began at the Old Town House made up of a platoon of police, the Salem Cadet Band, GAR veterans and citizens who marched to the rectory on Summer Street, where Lieutenant Rollins joined the parade in an automobile driven by Mr. George E. Nichols. At Abbot Hall, Reverend Rollins was greeted by a standing ovation lasting over five minutes. The festivities began outdoors, with people gathering at the south end of the building and the speakers lining up on the steps. A cold, raw wind off the ocean developed and a heavy mist turned into pouring rain, but the people stood there for over an hour listening to the remarks of the speakers. Finally, rain fell so heavily that the festivities were moved inside.

The chaplain presented Comrade Thomas Swasey of Post 32 GAR a small American flag that he had "carried over the top." Chaplain Rollins, on behalf of the town of Marblehead, was presented with a gold watch and fob with the inscription, "Presented to Chaplain Rollins by the citizens of

Marblehead for distinguished service rendered to his country in the world war." The festivities ended with the singing of "Marblehead Forever" and "The Star-Spangled Banner."

The Armistice

The following is a letter from Sergeant W.A.F. Power, son of Stephen Woodfin and Jennie Dwight Chin Power, written to the people of the town telling how the news of the signing of the Armistice was received at the French town where he was at the time.[52] Since late in July 1918, he had been suffering from rheumatism, but prior to that, since February he had been constantly in and out of the trenches.

Chatel Guyon, France
November 11, 1918

Dears:

Well, according to all reports today it's all over. Report after report has come in and to such an extent that everyone has accepted it as a fact. You probably received the news as soon as we. But oh, what a demonstration is going on outside. French and American soldiers and civilians, men and women, grownups and children marching themselves lame and shouting themselves hoarse through all the streets and alleys of this town, banging the pans and cymbals, blowing bugles and horns and waving flags of all the Allies. And how the Stars and Stripes does stand out from all the group. The sidewalks are covered with weeping and laughing old men and women, joyful because of the end of the war, yet sad because someone will not return. Now and then a French hunter returning through town, stops and seeing the demonstration looks on for a while and then fires several shots from his shotgun into the air. This gives the crowds new vigor and they start afresh.

One very funny incident I saw was this. The crowds were in another part of town when down the street we heard 1-2-3-4, 1-2-3-4; we looked and up the street came a group of cripples, each walking on two crutches, stretching across the road in double rank and marching in true military style, 16 in all. On they came, keeping perfect time and as they got abreast of us the one evidently with "beaucoup francs" gave the command "Squad right—march," and they wheeled and split into a column of squads up over the sidewalk and into a café, where evidently the "one" was going to "set them up."

We are all awaiting for tomorrow's papers to get the official statement, but nevertheless we have begun to think of getting home and of how long it will be. But it can't be long now. What a wonderful sight the coast line of "God's country" will be when it finally pops up over the horizon. But even then in the extreme moments of joy one will not be able to forget the ones who saw the coast disappear, never to reappear to their eyes.

W.A.F. Power

Mr. Elmer Bray Brown of Marblehead was in the navy from April 15, 1918, to March 14, 1919, and trained at Camp Charleston, South Carolina, as a machinist's mate. He was working on aviation motor machines and was stationed at the Naval Air Station at Key West, Florida, when he wrote in his daily journal on November 11, 1918, "The war has ended." Elmer was the "last native son" of World War I when he died in Marblehead in 1995 at the age of 101 years and ten months.

The War Is Over!

THAT MEANS

BETTER BREAD
CRACKERS of QUALITY
BUY LINDSEY'S

Advertisement for N.B. Lindsey Baking Company. *Courtesy of* Marblehead Messenger, *June 28, 1918. Author's collection.*

Service medals, Elmer B. Brown. *Courtesy of Clifford Brown Sr.*

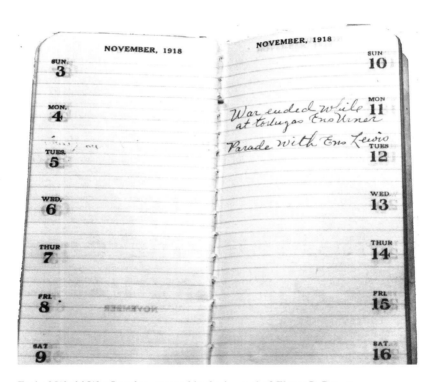

End of World War I as documented in the journal of Elmer B. Brown, Marblehead. *Courtesy of Clifford Brown Sr.*

Discharge papers of Elmer B. Brown. *Courtesy of Clifford Brown Sr.*

RETURNING HOME

Governor Samuel McCall of Massachusetts told all cities and towns to plan for celebrations for their men returning from the war. As usual, Marblehead citizens began to prepare early for these events.

On Monday night, November 11, 1918, the town held a gala celebration that was touted as the "largest in town history." It was carried out by the Live Wire Committee with only a few hours in which to prepare.[53] The news of the Armistice came suddenly, and Marblehead wanted to celebrate quickly. The parade route was one of the longest in the town's history, being over five miles long, heading from Pleasant Street to Atlantic Avenue all the way to Wyman Road to Bubier Road back to Atlantic Avenue. From there it went along Commercial Street to Gregory to Lee to Hooper and on to Washington Street, down State Street to Front and Franklin Streets and up Washington to Mugford, Elm and Spring Streets. It returned to the YMCA by Washington Street to Pleasant Street. This route was so strenuous that many participants had to drop out along the way and become spectators; nevertheless, it was a splendid parade. Almost everyone marching held an American flag, and the route was once again lit up with red sticks. There were bands, automobiles, decorated wagons pulled by horses and, the highlight for the children, "Master Billy Bryant" and his pet pony Snookie, with Shirley Gilbert riding beside him in a decorated pony cart. Upon

RECORD OF SERVICE

Name *Stewart Smith.* Serial No. *385110*
Co. and Reg. or Arm *310 Aero Squadron.*
Residence *28 Beacon St.* Kin *Mr. + Mrs. C. H. Smith*
Born - place *Marblehead* Age at enl. *22 yr. 6 mo.*
Eyes *Brown* Hair *Dk. brown* Complexion *Ruddy* Height *5 ft. 9 in.*
Married or Single *Single* Enl. period *first*
Prior Service

Enlisted or Drafted *Drafted* Reported *May 31, 1918.*
Assigned to *310 Aero Squadron.* at
Discharged H.D., Dis. not recommended, D.D.
for re-enlistment
Character *Excellent.*
Military Record *Foreign Service A.E.F. Left U.S.A. July 31, 1918.*

Battles *None*

Wounds or other injuries received in action *None*

Medal of honor - action and date
Certificate of merit - action and date
D.S.C. D.S.M. W.C.A.
Other medals and foreign decorations
Occupation *Sheet Metal Worker.*
Military qualifications
Record of conviction by Courts-Martial

Company Punishment

Transfers

Service with A.E.F. *July 31, 1918 to Dec. 2, 1918.*
Sailed from U.S. *July 31, 1918* Arrived at Port overseas
Sailed from Port overseas Arrived at Port on return

Record of service for Stewart Smith, Marblehead. *Author's collection.*

Honorable Discharge from The United States Army

TO ALL WHOM IT MAY CONCERN:

This is to Certify, That *Stewart Smith*
†385110 Private 310th Aero Squadron
THE UNITED STATES ARMY, as a TESTIMONIAL of HONEST and FAITHFUL
SERVICE. is hereby HONORABLY DISCHARGED from the military service of the
UNITED STATES by reason of *Letter H.S. S. of M.A. November 29, 1918*
Said *Stewart Smith* was born
in *Marble Head*, in the State of *Massachusetts.*
When enlisted he was *22½* years of age and by occupation a *Sheet Metal Worker.*
He had *brown* eyes, *Dk. Brown* hair, *Ruddy* complexion, and
was *5* feet *9* inches in height.
Given under my hand at *Air Service Depot Garden City, N.Y.* this
18 day of *December*, one thousand nine hundred and *eighteen.*

Washington, D. C. APR 23 1919
Paid $60 under 4.
February 24th, 191 .
C. E.
Major, O. A.

W. Noad
Lieutenant Colonel, U.S.A.
Commanding.

Form No. 525, A. G. O.
Oct. 9-18.

Honorable discharge papers for Stewart Smith, Marblehead. *Author's collection.*

ENLISTMENT RECORD.

Name: *Stewart Smith*   Grade: *Private*

Enlisted, or Inducted, *May 31st*, 1918, at *Swampscott, Massachusetts*

Serving in *First*   enlistment period at date of discharge.

Prior service: * *None*

Noncommissioned officer: *No*

Marksmanship, gunner qualification or rating: † *None*

Horsemanship: *Not Mounted*

Battles, engagements, skirmishes, expeditions: *None*

Knowledge of any vocation: *Machinist*

Wounds received in service: *None*

Physical condition when discharged: *Good*

Typhoid prophylaxis completed *June 19, 1918*

Paratyphoid prophylaxis completed *June 19, 1918*

Married or single: *Single*

Character: *Excellent*

Remarks *Foreign Service A.E.F. Left U.S.A. July 31, 1918. Returned Dec. 2nd, 1918. Soldier entitled to wear one Blue Sleeve Chevrons. Soldier entitled to travel pay to Swampscott, Mass. Par 1248 under Act of April 17, 1918. M. C O 45 W.D. 1918.*

Signature of soldier: *Stewart Smith*

Paid in full $ 119.05
on Final Statement

*Alfred G. Wayhurst
Captain Air Service*
Commanding *3rd Air Squadron*

S.J.D. Marshall 1st S.

Right: Enlistment record for Stewart Smith, Marblehead. *Author's collection.*

Below: Victory parade, 1919, Washington Street, Marblehead. *Courtesy of Marblehead Historical Commission, Abbot Hall, Marblehead, MA, object ID 2001-070-0481. www. marbleheadhistory.com.*

returning to Monument Park, there were many speeches and lots of singing of patriotic songs until about 10:00 p.m., when things began to quiet down.

"Our Boys That Are Drafted In"
By Mary E. Harris of Marblehead

I know they belong to the rank and file,
    Our boys that are drafted in;
But they serve their God and their country's flag,
    Our boys that are drafted in.

No coward's blood runs in their veins,
    Our boys that are drafted in;
They will do their best for a righteous cause,
    Our boys that are drafted in.

They are soldiers of the cross,
    Our boys that are drafted in;
And their feet will tread Gethsemane,
    Our boys that are drafted in.

The shot and shell of the trench's hell,
    Wait our boys that are drafted in;
But the uniform covers hearts of gold, when worn
    By our boys that are drafted in.

When the general roll is called on high,
    And the blocks are squared by the Master's eye,
They will get their due from their Comrade true,
    Our boys that are drafted in.

O thou pitying Christ, look down and save
    Our boys that are drafted in;
By thy pierced hand, by thy wondrous love,
    Save our boys that are drafted in.

Printed in the Marblehead Messenger, *February 15, 1918*

Chapter 7

LETTERS HOME

There were many letters published in the *Marblehead Messenger* from the boys serving their country, all telling of their experiences in the service and instructing their friends and families at home not to worry. The young men also wanted to be sure their families were taken care of while they were away. They would have allotments from their pay sent home to family. John U. Barrowclough wrote to his mother in February 1917, telling her that he had opened an account and if she were "ever pushed for money" to remember that "the whole blamed shooting match is at your disposal."[54] There were also many thank-you letters sent to the women of Marblehead in appreciation of all their hard work at home in supporting the soldiers.

HOLIDAYS

For most of the boys, their service experience was the first time that they were away from home for a holiday. According to most of the boys, the government provided food and entertainment for the men. Edward Evans wrote a letter to his parents around Thanksgiving from his camp in France:[55]

England. Oct 16, 1918

Dear Sister Received your last
letter all right and was glad to
hear from you, got your money
order day after pay day so have
plenty of coin for a while. Got
Peters and Elsies letter all right
and I see he has trouble with
his car yet, also hear that our
~~boat is doing~~ better this year.
Tell him not to sell her, because
I might get a chance to try it
out myself next summer. Guess
~~Harvey~~ Mac is ~~done~~ doing some sailing this summer by the looks
of the records, and I guess he
will do some this ~~winter~~ as I
understand he has ~~done~~ joined
the navy. Take it from me when
we get back and the bunch gets
together we will have some times.
By Elsies letter I see Harriet
and her are still some sports.

(2)

Harriet must feel lost not to
have the bunch to wait on at
Jack's Store, although Jake is as
good as the bunch. Tell Jack to
have a good store on hand
when I get back. Tell Jake to
be carefull with that gun of his
and not shoot any birds like Bill
merrill did, but I dont think there
will be any sea birds left if you
let Jake loose. Am glad to hear
you are having such fine weather at home as it is raining
or unsettled weather all the time.
never felt better in my life than
I do now, hope mother and Ralph
are also well.

your Brother
Stewart.

EDMUND EAST??
1st Lieut. A. ?.

Letter home from England to his
sister from Stewart Smith, October
16, 1918. *Author's collection.*

108

Letters Home

"Somewhere in France"

Dear Mother:

One more week spent in the same old camp in France, not knowing if we will be here another week or not. There are only a few more days to Thanksgiving. We are going to have quite a time here although I don't believe there are many of the boys who don't wish they were back home and eating their dinners with their own families. Nevertheless I hope you will enjoy your part of it and I will try to do my best.

There is something for which we should be able to give thanks from the bottom of our hearts, and that is that though we are separated by a number of thousands of miles and the broad Atlantic, we still have those at home whose prayers are with us; we are even praying for you; also we can be thankful that though we are separated we are all in good health and even though I am a fighting man in a great world war, I am still alive. You people at home should be especially thankful that you are living in the greatest and noblest country in the whole world. I myself could not see what a wonderful country it is until I have traveled half-way around the world, and seen many people.

What we consider in the old United States as absolute necessities are in this old world luxuries. You can imagine a Frenchman eating a piece of white bread with apparently more relish than we would bestow on a piece of nice chocolate cream pie.

We are going to have a regular New England Thanksgiving dinner with all the fixings and a minstrel show in the evening. So you can see that Uncle Sam is trying to do his best by us.

Hoping you have a good time Thanksgiving and Christmas, I am

Yours with love,
Edward.

Edward wrote a second letter to his father adding a little more description of the holidays overseas:

Dear Father:

I don't know whether I thanked you for the tobacco or not. If not, I will do so now. It sure was great, but it is now all gone, unfortunately for me. I am now smoking French cigars; they taste as though they had been soaked in soapsuds and kerosene.

We are preparing for a grand Thanksgiving celebration, but we cannot arrange for a Christmas celebration as yet, as we do not know where we will be, but even if we are on the Swiss border, in Italy or the front line trenches in Flanders, you can leave it to old F Battery to start something. It may be some harmless sports among ourselves or we may enjoy ourselves by sending Christmas greetings to the Boches via a number of French "75's," using high explosives or gas shells for our cards, or we may even consolidate with the infantry and hike to Berlin and present our compliments to Kaiser Bill personally.

We have a grand program for Thanksgiving. All kinds of races and sports in the morning, a regular turkey dinner at noon, topped with a couple of glasses of Madeira or champagne, a big football game in the afternoon; I say big because each side has 100 men, making 200 players on the field at once with four footballs going at once; I imagine they will have to have a couple of field hospital units there and ready for business and then to top off with a grand minstrel show in the evening by members of F Battery, assisted by the Y.M.C.A. piano and the full regimental band. All members of the regiment are invited; doughnuts and coffee will be served in the refreshment tent.

Well, Pa, write often and if you can send a little "Edgeworth" as I have a nice little pipe that I use for American tobacco only.

Hoping you enjoy the holidays, I am

Your kid,
Ed

MISSING FAMILY HAPPENINGS

Life went on at home, and the boys missed weddings, births and deaths in the town. They only learned of these happenings by letters from home. The following letter is from Leonard O. Peach to his mother showing just that. His grandmother, Sarah Collyer Peach, died on October 30, 1917:[56]

"On Active Service with the American Expeditionary Forces"
December 4, 1917

Letters Home

My Dear Mother:

Just a line to let you know I am all right and feeling fine except that it is growing very cold. I am very sorry to hear that Grandma has died. I would like to have seen her once more.

It has been so long since I sent the last letter I will tell you all I can for it may be a very long time before you get another. We are waiting orders to break up camp. If we go on trains it will take about three days, but if we go over the road it will take at least a month. Of course, the next camp will be just back of the front, in a small village.

For the past few weeks everything has been going on just the same until Thanksgiving. We had that day off and in the morning Battery D played Battery F in a game of football and we lost 20 to 0, but it was a good game. For dinner we had turkey and everything that goes with it. We also had plum pudding. At night we had songs and dances by the fellows and the band played a few songs. Then we all lined up for cider and doughnuts, but I didn't think much of the cider. I could have eaten more, but there I won't kick. We were told that it probably would be the last time that we would have a chance to enjoy ourselves, as we expect to be in the trenches before Christmas.

I have received all the papers and letters that you sent me. The Christmas box you sent is here and I was very glad to get it as it cheered me up. Please tell everybody who put presents in for me that I thank them very much and would write them a letter, but the censor has given another order that we can send only two letters a week. You needn't be afraid to write what you wish as the censor hasn't opened our letters so far.

I am going to save the stockings you sent for my rubber boots, as they say if we don't keep our feet warm we will have trench feet, and when we once get them we may as well go home. I got my steel helmet the other day and now am waiting for my gas mask.

I don't get much chance to go to church, but I think about it.

I don't know what to say for I have received mail from everybody today and when the box came with the watch, I had to jump up with a yell.

Everybody is getting a box today as we are told there are six hundred sacks of mail in. We only receive mail once every two weeks. A fellow has just come in and says more mail has come in. The men are working night and day trying to get all the mail to us before we leave. I think I have received everything you have sent so far.

We still have a few flowers in bloom, but they will soon go, for the weather is very damp and cold. It seems to go right through one's clothes, and if we didn't keep working we would freeze.

Now please don't get worried about me, for if I should get sick I will get someone to write.

Goodbye until I reach the next camp.

Your loving son,
Leonard

NOT SO MONOTONOUS AS I THOUGHT

Mr. Fred Robinson, who served with the Harvard Hospital Unit, wrote his mother and father in September 1917 telling as much he could of the Germans bombing a hospital in France. He enlisted May 7, 1917, in Harvard Unit, No. 5, Medical Corps, and was the first Marblehead man in the war to cross the ocean:[57]

"Somewhere in France,"
September 17, 1917

Dear Mother and Father:

In my last letter, written day before yesterday, I said that the place here was terribly monotonous, and that I would be very much ashamed of myself if I should have come home without being any nearer shell-fire than I am now. But it seems that I was laboring under a very wrong vision of things, for since I wrote my other letter we have been raided by German aero planes, resulting in an appreciable number of killed and a good many wounded. It is against the rules to give the exact number of casualties, but I presume that the whole affair has been published in the papers.

You remember I told you that for the last few days German aero-planes have been reconnoitering about this vicinity both at night and at day. They always come at such heights that they can be seen distinctly only with a powerful field glass; but when one sees a speck in the sky and wonders whether it is a Fritz or one of our own, the question is very quickly settled by the booming of the

112

anti-aircraft, and by the little clouds of pure white smoke that make their appearance suddenly and without warning all over the sky. The sound of the explosions does not reach earth for a good many moments after it occurs.

It is an extremely weird sight to stand watching a perfectly clear, crystal blue sky and then to see a white cloud appear there, and then another and another, each looking for all the world as if they were right at home there and had sailed from the horizon. At night the place of the little clouds is taken by bright red flashes that resemble very much shooting stars or those high rockets that simply flash and go out that one sees on the Fourth of July.

But last Tuesday night was the night as far as thrills and excitement went. The moon, about full, had just risen over the low hill at the back of the hospital, and all the world around was as bright as day. We tried to make the camp as dark as possible by turning out all the electric lights, and by using just a few other lights as were necessary for doing the work. Taps had blown about half an hour before and I was in my bunk almost asleep. Then all of a sudden away off to the south I heard a boom of heavy guns that I knew were anti aircraft. The report of an anti aircraft gun is heavier and of a deeper intonation than any other of the big guns that I have ever heard, so this, coupled with the suspicions of everyone that we would be raided at some time, convinced me that Fritz was about and that it would not be very long before the dirty work would begin. Everybody was outside their tents anxiously gazing into the sky, but nothing of an aeroplane could either be seen or heard. There was a short and sharp z-z-z-t, followed by a thunderous explosion. Even then very few of us realized the danger of the situation, but stood around craning our necks up where we knew the Fritz must be and just waited for events to happen. And they certainly did happen.

After the first explosion, there came three more in quick succession, then a slight lull, and then another explosion, and lull and then another explosion. At every explosion we could hear whizzing of shrapnel and could see the flash of sparks. Two other fellows and myself were only about fifty feet away when the bomb struck, so you see we have quite a first-hand knowledge of the whole affair. Still, however, a surprisingly small number got the "wind up" as they express it over here, the reason being that no one really realized just to what extent we were in danger. It was all over in less than five minutes and everyone ran around to see just what danger had been done. And then for the first time the real horror and ghastliness of the whole affair dawned on us. At least that was my own experience, for up to that time I had looked upon it as a pretty good way of breaking up the terrible monotony that we have had here for the month or two. But when I saw the dead bodies being carried off and the wounded being treated—some of the sights are more than I would have the heart to describe, such as the sight of a human being blown absolutely to shreds—I and everybody else realized that this was certainly a bit of war, and war of the meanest and most despicable type.

But for this little affair—for it is little compared to what is going on at the front line—it is all over now, and the camp has resumed much of its former repose and monotony. As for myself I am safe and sound, and with the good luck that usually follows me, expect to continue to be so "for the duration" as they say over here. So by all means do not worry, for I am sure that I am not, and you know I am the most directly concerned. At best, occurrences such as that which happened the other night must be very rare, for they are of little or no military importance. So let it drop out of your mind, and send me some more of Girdler Stacey's kisses, for my stomach is the only important thing to me now.

Remember me to all
Your loving son,
Fred Robinson

Capture of a German Town

This letter written by Corporal Clarence Wilson of Company C, 104th Infantry, to Mrs. Walter Smethurst was rather unique, as according to the *Marblehead Messenger* it was written on German paper found in a captured town following a big drive.[58]

"Somewhere in France"
September 14, 1918

Dear Emma:
*   Just a few lines to let you know that I am alive and well and hope this letter finds you all the same. You probably know by this time that we have been "over the top" again, but believe me, this one was twice as easy as the last one.*

On a dark and rainy night we moved into the support trenches and slept there until early in the morning. All the time we were there the artillery was showing the Boches what it could do and, believe me, they did some fine work, because when we went over we met very little resistance and what there was came from machine guns placed on the edge of the woods to stop our advance until the main party had more of a chance to get away.

In our sector there were plenty of woods to go through, but very few Boches for us to take prisoners or kill.

In our turn in the lead we had a sight that would make any fellow feel good and that was a plateau with six or seven towns in it and in the one we went there were plenty of German supplies. I ate some of the German bread with and without jam. Without the jam the bread tastes like sawdust, but it went down just the same.

Most everybody got a German sweater and blanket. The French people who were in the town when we took it had been there since the beginning of the war. Maybe they were not glad to see us come and make them free once again.

I am writing this letter on some German paper, using an envelope and pencil that were found in some of their quarters.

I will close now with love to all.

Corp. Clarence Wilson

"Marblehead"
By Elva D. Perkins

M is for the Million lads to France already gone,
A is for the Armor that when given a chance they don,
R is for the Railroad which took them from our town,
B is for the Barracks, like the soldier's khaki brown,
L is for the Letters we look for day by day,
E is for the Enemy they hope to drive away,
H is for the Hours spent in longing for world peace,
E is for the Eager ones whose prayers do never cease
A is for America, the land for which they fight,
D is for our Dear ones whom we pray for day and night.

Printed in the Marblehead Messenger, *January 18, 1918*

Chapter 8

WOUNDED AND KILLED

All the men who served in the armed services during World War I were called heroes upon their return to their hometowns. Unfortunately, Marblehead lost six men due to the war, and many were wounded or gassed. The six men who received Gold Stars were Lieutenant Charles H. Evans, John Alexis Roundy, Irving E. Brown, John McGee, William F. Farry and Christian S. Christensen. George W. Morrill of Swampscott, who was part of the Tenth Deck Division, also lost his life.

USS *Covington*

Several Marblehead men were aboard the USS *Covington* when it was sunk by a submarine in July 1918. Early in the evening of July 1, 1918, the ship was steaming westward from Brest, France, in a U.S. Navy convoy of eight transports, escorted by seven destroyers. They were bound for the United States after having delivered more troops to France. The sea was calm with good visibility, and all the ships were zigzagging and on the lookout for German submarines. At 9:12 p.m., a torpedo was launched and detonated against the port side of the *Covington*. The explosion was below the forward smokestack and blew open the ship's forward boiler room, causing the ship to stop and begin to list to the port. Six crew members were killed as a result of the explosion.

The first letter home telling of the catastrophe was sent by Roger Ward:[59]

"On Active Service
July 18, 1918

Dear Ma:

I suppose you have been wondering where I am and if we are all well. As you know we are somewhere in France, and as Ensign Steele cabled you, I guess you are not worrying much. I hope not.

In the first place I want Mary to do me a favor and send a nicely worded letter to the Messenger *telling of the treatment we received from Ensign Steele. He took the trouble to come over to see me and saw that I got a good razor and outfit, toothbrush and paste, money to buy necessary articles and also cabled home to the folks. She can't word it any too good and I cannot show my appreciation and thanks for what he had done for me. In that way his folks and all his friends will know that I show some respect for a friend from Marblehead who helped me out in a time of need.*

I saw Mr. Graves, the letter carrier's son, the other day and he is feeling and looking fine. When you see his dad you can tell him.

We are now supplied with clothing and are no worse for the experience we went through. It was a terrific explosion and happened just as it was getting dark. When the ship was hit it looked as if it would go down in a minute. We took our boats and were picked up in short order and taken to port. I lost everything but the clothes I had on, and my dress blue jumper. Your picture I was keeping in such good shape and all the rest of my things have gone.

It looks as if we would stay here. I think it will be a long day before I see Marblehead again, but as long as everybody is well I don't regret it, as I may get a chance to get a good whack at some German in revenge for what they have done to me. I want to tell you that our gun crew sunk the submarine before we left our ship and when it was hit all hands cheered to think that she had the same, but still worse medicine than we.

I don't know where I will be stationed as yet, as we are getting spread all over France, but as yet I have not been assigned. I will write again as soon and as often as I can.

Now don't forget to give Ensign Steele a good write-up. Tell how we were landed in a French port after being picked up by destroyers and taken care

*of there, and how he tended to my needs. Tell Roy Proctor and his wife that
we crossed the ocean just once too often and the old Kaiser got hit. In return
his servants are resting at the bottom of the ocean.*

*Tell Father Monahan that I saved that soldier's and sailor's prayer book
and that I went down below deck after being torpedoed just for that and I
now treasure it more than ever. I will close now hoping to hear from you
soon and also to hear that all are in the best of health.*

Sincerely your loving son,

Roger

Edmund F. Glover Jr. was also a crew member from Marblehead aboard
the USS *Covington* and wrote to his parents telling of his escape from death
when the boat sank.[60]

"On Active Duty" July 4, 1918

Dear Ma and Dad:

*I am with Mr. Steele again. The good old ship went down the first of
July. There are only two or three lost as far as they know just now. I hope
they find everybody, because we were all like brothers on her.*

*There was no trouble in getting off her; she stayed up until the next day.
So you see there was plenty of time for all of us to get off. The boys that
they think were lost were all new to the fire room and did not know how
to get up. There were a lot who had their faces and hands cut, but not very
badly. Harold Hall and Roger Ward are fine and also myself, so you have
nothing to worry about. I will be all right.*

*Mr. Steele has fitted out Hall, Ward and myself with a toothbrush and
paste, a shaving brush and cream, soap and also a razor and fifty francs.
So you can see that we have one good old friend with us. We have all been
fitted out with new clothes. My old suit was pretty well worn out and I was
thinking all the time about buying a new one, so you see it pays to wait and
see what is hanging up for you.*

*I was sound asleep in my hammock and heard a bang. I knew it was
time for me to get up. I jumped out and got my clothes on in a hurry, but
did not have time to look around for my shoes after that. I made one grand
rush for the top side and found Hall and Ward alright. All the officers were*

there. They said "well boys, let's get going." So we started letting the boats and rafts down and everything went off finely.

I was in the water for two hours but did not mind that, the water was great, it was just like over to Back Beach. One of the doctors was in the raft with me and he said, "What is the matter, can't anyone sing?" Well we started and had him laughing the whole time until we reached the beach. He said, "that's fine boys." Well Ma, I am as happy as I can be, but I wish that it was near New York so that I could get home to see you. But don't you care. I will come just as soon as I can and hope to find you just as happy as you were the night I left you at the depot.

I am at Mr. Steele's room now. I am going to the show tonight. Today is the Fourth of July, but you hardly know it over here. They had a parade this morning. It was very good. I saw a lot of soldiers from the front. They looked very good.

Well, Ma, I can't think of any more just now, so will close. Give my love to Sadie and Chester, Mrs. Munroe, Alice and Leon, Mrs. Wilkins and the whole family.

Love to all again, from your loving son, Ed.

The Live Wire Committee, which was formed in Marblehead to aid the men and their families, voted to send seventy-five dollars to Ensign Everett V. Steele to reimburse him for the money he expended in aiding the Marblehead men on the *Covington*. Everett was born on October 22, 1897, in Marblehead, son of Jonathan and Minnie Bennett Steele.[61] He served in the navy in both World War I and World War II. He married Priscilla E. Whalen on June 11, 1924,[62] and died in Whittier, California, on January 3, 1980.

A Local Hero

Alfred R. (Gunboat) Smith received a medal of honor from the French government for his bravery in battle. He was the first Marbleheader to gain distinction while fighting the Germans. Alfred was born in Marblehead, the grandson of Mrs. Lorenzo Smith, and graduated from the public schools, taking up the mason's trade, which he learned from his uncle, Mr. Frank Smith. As soon as the war broke out on April 6, 1917, he went to Salem and enlisted in Battery D, 101st Regiment Light Artillery, at the age of twenty-three. He trained at Camp Curtis Guild in Boxford, Massachusetts, and was sent to France in September 1917. While he was under fire in the sector known as Chemin de Dames, the lanyard of the cannon broke. According to the *Boston Globe* of April 15, 1915, when the lanyard broke he sprang forward, saying, "Keep on loading her boys, I will see that she is fired." Standing in full view of the enemy, he continued firing the gun until it became so hot it burned his hands. He pulled the lanyard 207 times in forty-five minutes.[63]

A few weeks prior to this experience, he had written a letter home to his friend Chief Engineer John T. Adams complaining of the lack of excitement and that his troop had not been under fire as yet:

"On Active Service," March 15, 1918

My Dear Friend Mr. Adams:

Just a few lines to let you know that I am well and am in the best of health. We are now on the firing line and believe me we have had some exciting times since we struck here. The first scrap our battery was in was a corker. I am what they call number one man on the gun. My job is to set the range scale and pull the lanyard. These French "75" guns very often blow up, so they have a long lanyard on it and everybody ducks behind sand bags and then I pull and she goes off. So I had to stand right side of her and fire 202 more shots. Believe me it was some noise and I couldn't hear for two days. We fired 207 shots in an hour; the nearest piece to us fired 164. So you see my gun crew had a fine record.

After we got through firing, the lieutenant came up and said to me, "Smith, you certainly showed Marblehead spirit tonight." And I said, "Sir, you put a crew of Marblehead boys on the d—d old gun and we'll take her right into Berlin." And I believe we would, too. This reads like a story, don't it, Chief? But it is honest. Say, Chief, I wish you were here to see the aeroplane fights. Every day and at night the Boche machines drop bombs and some land pretty close to us. We have been through two kinds of gas, tear and chlorine gas, but we are very speedy about putting on our gas masks.

You ought to hear what is said about the old First Massachusetts Regiment, Chief. The French have cited us twice for bravery and coolness under fire. And that entitles us to what is called a distinguished cord, which hangs over your shoulder.

Once every three nights I have to do guard duty and for two hours on a stretch. And believe me, Chief, when those star shells and flare lights get agoing and the aeroplanes go buzzing by it makes a lad think a heap of home and a bed, and the last but not least three square meals.

What do you think of Massachusetts taking away the $10 a month state pay from the volunteers and still letting the draftees have it? It seems pretty mean and we over here, the old First Massachusetts Field Artillery feel pretty sore at old Massachusetts for it.

Well Chief, I will write again some time to you and good old Sam Sweet, give him my best regards.

Alfred (Gunboat) Smith

In another letter, Alfred told of how a while later they were even in a hotter battle ground where he was acting as gunner's corporal for three days, from April 7 to 10, 1918. On April 10 at four o'clock in the morning the Germans bombarded them, and "little Alfred" awoke in a nice bed with an honest-to-goodness USA girl leaning over him and asking if he was all right. She told him he was dreaming about boats and fried clams. "Ain't it funny what a lad will say when he gets knocked daffy."[64]

Alfred sent a rather humorous letter to his grandmother on June 2, 1918, and in it he told her, "Ever since I got wounded I have at least twelve letters from girls who saw my picture in the Post. One was from Vermont, one from New Hampshire and the rest around Boston. One from Dorchester sent me her picture and believe me she is some queen." He went on to tell his grandmother that the division was going to have a big review and he was going to get a medal. "Gee, it all makes me sick; why, Gram, if you or anybody was on that job that day, they would have done the same thing. I have been presented with a wound stripe and a young French girl sewed it on my arm."[65]

CHARLES H. EVANS

The first Marblehead soldier to lose his life was Second Lieutenant Charles Herbert Evans, son of Joseph and Hannah Martin Graves Evans of 32 Maverick Street, who was born on March 11, 1887 in Marblehead.[66] He was educated in the Marblehead public schools, graduating in 1905. Following his graduation, he was employed by the Boston and Maine Railroad as a clerk in Lynn, later transferring to Beverly and then to Chelsea. He married Mary E. Salkins on March 15, 1910, in Marblehead.[67] He did not wait for the draft but started preparing himself for service by studying evenings preparing for the examination for the officers' school in Plattsburg, New York. He passed his course of study and entered the school on May 8, 1917. On August 15, 1917, he received his commission to second lieutenant and was immediately assigned to duty at Camp Devens in Ayer, Massachusetts, from which he was transferred to Camp Bartlett in Westfield, Massachusetts, where he was assigned to Company K, 103rd U.S. Infantry. He sailed overseas with his company on September 23, 1917, arriving in England on October 17. Charles and his company were involved in the famous Chateau Thierry Drive in France. He was killed on July 20, 1918, during an assault on the Etrepilly Plateau near Bouresches, France.[68]

Second Lieutenant Charles H. Evans, killed in action, July 20, 1918. *Photo from Live Wire Committee publication, circa 1919.*

Wounded and Killed

While serving in France, he sent letters home to his friends and family telling of his experiences in France. On February 25, 1918, he wrote his friend Mr. Everett Bridgeo telling of his life in France:[69]

France, February 26, 1918

Everett, Old Scout:

How are you and all the boys? I haven't heard much about Marblehead except in mother's letters and the Messenger, which comes O.K. What are you doing now? When do you expect to be drafted? It is quiet over here. I am in a large cave dug out of limestone and large enough for 1,000 men. This place is all cut up with shell holes, trenches and barbed wire.

The air is full of aeroplanes, both French and German, also American and they have scraps every day. Some nights with the anti-aircraft guns shelling them. The other day they brought down several German planes and I went over to see the occupants, one major and the other first lieutenant; they were some men. It is great to have large shells bursting all around. Have to "work" if you want to keep your head.

Is there the same crowd on the first train as usual or have many of them been drafted?

Drop me a line once in a while.

C.H. Evans

On February 16, 1918, he wrote to his mother telling her about foiling a German attack:[70]

France, February 16, 1918

This is the first chance I have had to write. I started several letters, but did not get time to finish them. I have just come out of the front line trenches and had a great time. They shelled us every day and put over gas but it did no great damage. I got a little in my left eye and it is quite painful. I think it will come out O.K.

The last night I was in the trenches the Germans made a raid on my sector, but I cleaned them up. There were about 18 and they threw wizbangs, bombs and hand grenades, but they were all too high. It was some fun while it lasted and I enjoyed it. They did not try it again. I think they got more than they expected. I don't think they know that there are American troops here in this part and they have been trying to find out what is going on here.

I expect to get my 7 day leave soon and am going to Paris if possible. Don't worry about me, I am OK.

Love,

Charles
Can you get some of those Red Cross woolen socks? I cannot get any here and I am all out.
C

The news that every family dreaded came to his parents in a telegram from the War Department on August 5, 1918: "Deeply regret to inform you that Lt. Charles H. Evans, Infantry, is officially reported as killed in action, July 20, 1918. Signed McCain, Adj. Gen."

The following article was in the *Marblehead Messenger* on August 9, 1918:

The war was brought very closely home to Marblehead this week when news of the death of Lieutenant Charles H. Evans, killed in France, July 20, the first Marbleheader to fall in action in the great conflict across the water, reached his parents here and was later communicated to the townspeople. According to his parents, "he was anxious to go and prepared himself."

Deepest regret was felt by all, friends, acquaintances and townspeople for this splendid young man, whose life passed out in the field of battle while he was valiantly doing his part to make the "world safe for democracy." This regret was tempered by pride, however, just pride felt by both his parents and the town as a whole, for this young officer in our army abroad was a true soldier in every sense of the word, and up to the last minute of his life conducted himself as a gentlemen and a soldier of the highest type, and proved himself true to his early training and to the military traditions of the old town for which he hailed.

His letters home were particularly characteristic of the men for they always carried a message of cheer to his parents and generally closed with "don't worry, I am all right." And all this, despite the hardships endured in the front line, where he had suffered frozen feet and had also been through the terrible experience of being "gassed."

In his passing on his parents lost a son in whom they had reason to feel the highest pride and the town a citizen who, through his death, has brought to its shield of honor added fame. The people of the town displayed their flags at half-mast in honor of his memory.

His mother received a letter in October 1918 from Chaplain A.G. Butzer regarding the particulars of the death of her son. The letter explains that Lieutenant Evans died in the performance of his duty, meeting death bravely and without complaint, being instantly killed by a machine gun bullet. Naturally, Mrs. Evans wanted closure on her son's death, as any mother would, and sent a letter to the chaplain of his unit. She received the following reply:[71]

"On Active Service"
Oct. 4, 1918

My Dear Mrs. Evans:
Your communication addressed to the Chaplain of the 103rd Infantry reached me a couple of days ago, and I can well appreciate your motherly anxiety over the personal effects of your son, Lieut. Evans, who so gallantly gave his life for his country.

I got in touch with Lieut. Lane, who is now the commanding officer of the company to which your son belonged, and he informed me as follows.

All personal property, including whatever little trinkets he had were rolled up in his bedding roll, a complete inventory made of the same and the whole forwarded to the quartermaster department. In due time, it might be longer than due time, I fear, these personal effects which mean so much to you should reach you. If they fail to, write me again and I shall do all in my power to trace them.

I have come to the battalion since your son's death, but the officers who were near him when he fell tell me that he was killed while carrying out a mission prescribed by the battalion commander. He might have avoided death had he slighted his mission, but like the true soldier he was he went through terrific machine gun fire without a murmur or a fear and did the task he was ordered to do, but died soon after he had done so, a machine gun bullet of the enemy piercing his temple. Death was instantaneous with him and he was spared all pain and suffering.

I am also informed that he received a Christian and military burial by one of my Chaplain associates whose name at present I do not know, but I will endeavor to find out and get whatever other information from him that I can.

He was buried near Belleau. The exact location of the grave was undoubtedly sent to the Grave Registration Service and by writing them in Washington, D.C. you should receive it after a reasonable amount of time. The Chaplain is required to send all grave locations to this department, they make a record of them and then furnish the information to those who request it.

One of the boys showed me a picture he had of your son and my heart truly goes out to you in tenderest [sic] sympathy. You surely have laid a most precious sacrifice on the altar of country and of God.

As a Christian minister I beg you look unto Jesus, who is the Resurrection and the Life. May he comfort you in this hour of sorrow and cheer you all with the hope of a happy reunion in Heaven, where death and the war shall be no more.

I trust I have given you at least some of the information you crave. If I can be of further help, write me.

Sincerely,

Chaplain A.G. Butzer

Miss Jennie Glover Brown of Marblehead composed a verse dedicated to Lieutenant Evans:[72]

"In Memoriam"

Lieut. Charles H. Evans
Somewhere in France your hero lies,
His life a willing sacrifice,
Somewhere in France, mid shot and shell
Paving the way through awful Hell,
He fought the foes of right and truth,
Giving for us his strong, clean youth
Somewhere in France, in No Man's Land,
His boys pressed on a brave true band
Somewhere in France our moon looks down,

Wounded and Killed

On ruined home and shattered town,
While sunny skies and poppies red,
She brightens o'er the fields of dead
Each grave in France so far away
Means peace on earth this Christmas day
World-wide peace from shore to shore
While Prussian hate shall reign no more
To them, to us, has come "The Day"
For God has shown the righteous way.

Captain Evans's body was brought back home in August 1921, when a steamship brought the bodies of five hundred soldiers across the Atlantic to Hoboken, New Jersey. Upon the ship's arrival at the docks, a fire broke out, but all the bodies were removed safely from the ship. Memorial services over the bodies were held in New York, and then the bodies were sent to their respective towns. Lieutenant Evans's body arrived on the noon train on September 1 in a casket covered by a large American flag. He was taken to Undertaker George E. Nichols by Miss Katherine Sheehan of Salem, an employee of the U.S. Grave Registry Department who had accompanied the body from New York. Nichols took him to his parents' home on Maverick Street, and he was then taken to Abbot Hall the following day under the escort of the American Legion, there to lie in state until the funeral. There was a guard of honor of members of the American Legion, with Messrs. Everett Steele, R.W. Chase, David Snow, Thomas Trefry, Henry Collins, Frank Vincent, Carleton and Bradlee Brown, Ernest Gregory, W.H. Blackford, R.O. Brackett and Ralph Harris all performing this duty.

His funeral was held Sunday, September 4, 1921, at two o'clock. Reverend Leslie C. Greely, pastor of the Old North Church in Marblehead, officiated the service, which was attended by many townsfolk. The music was furnished by the Weber Quartet of Boston. Following the ceremony, the body was taken from the hall and placed on a caisson driven by four horses and was escorted to Waterside Cemetery, where Reverend Lyman Rollins officiated at the committal services. According to the news report, the cortege was an imposing one made up of a platoon of police, the American Legion band, the American Legion acting as the escort with the Grand Army, Sons of Veterans and Spanish War Veterans assisting.

IRVING EUGENE BROWN

The second Marblehead man to lose his life was Irving Eugene Brown, who died in Langres, France, at a base hospital in October 13, 1918, from pneumonia. His body was buried in a small cemetery near the base hospital. Irving was born in Marblehead on November 13, 1894, the son of Frank and Lizzie Roundy Brown.[73] His mother was the second cousin of John Alexis Roundy, who also lost his life in the war. Irving had one sister, Mrs. Henry Keenan, whose husband also served in France. Irving was educated in the Marblehead public schools. He was a shoe laster by trade and at the time of the draft was employed by the Parker Shoe Factory. He attended the Universalist Church of Marblehead and belonged to the Pickett Association and the Oko's Veteran Firemen.

Irving Eugene Brown, died in France October 12, 1918. *Photo from Live Wire Committee publication, circa 1919.*

Irving left Marblehead on April 29, 1918, for Camp Devens in response to the draft call, just nine days after marrying Miss Iris May Soper in Andover, Massachusetts, on July 6, 1918.[74] He left camp for France as a member of Battery B, 301st Infantry, and soon after his arrival was transferred to Company D, 167th Infantry, 42nd Division of Alabama. He had survived one of the great drives but fell ill on October 1, 1918. According to his friends, "He was of a cheerful disposition and had many friends, won by his unfailing good nature."[75]

JOHN ALEXIS ROUNDY

On January 17, 1919, John H. Roundy of 17 Elm Street received a telegram signed by Adjutant General Harris that his son John Alexis Roundy was missing in action and presumed dead. It was a dreadful shock to his family, as only that morning they had received a letter from Congressman Lufkin stating that as far as the records of the office showed, his son was alive and well. Mr. John G. Stevens of Marblehead contacted Congressman Peter Tague and had heard the same—he was alive and well. The Red Cross was unable to get any information about John but was trying to get in touch with the Paris office. To further confuse the matter, the government continued to send his monthly allotments to the family.

Mr. Roundy was born in Marblehead on April 20, 1895, the eldest son of John Henry and Sarah McDonald Roundy.[76] He attended the Marblehead public schools and attended Wentworth Institute in Boston to study architecture. He also took courses with the International Correspondence School. When he was drafted, he was employed with the Paine Shoe Company in town as a shoe assembler. He belonged to the Tenth Deck Division but was rejected for duty because he was underweight at the time the division was put into service. He was also rejected when first drafted and tried again on all four drafts, finally being accepted on April 29, 1918, and sent to Camp Devens. He continued on to France on July 6, 1918, with Company H, 111th Infantry, 28th Division. His draft registration card lists him with a medium build, blue eyes and dark hair. John saw service overseas on offensive sector in Meuse-Argonne and the defensive sector in Clermont (Lorraine).[77]

His father, confused by the mixed messages he was receiving, did not give up hope that he would later get word to the effect that it was all a mistake and his boy was alive and well. It made no sense to him that such prompt notification was given to the family of Irving E. Brown, who had been killed only a few days before his son. John's father wrote to the chaplain of his son's regiment in the hopes of getting more information regarding the fate of his son. The family took steps to collect the insurance money on the policy that his son took out in order to acquire more definite information regarding the fate of his son, supposing that the government would not pay the money without positive proof of his son's death. Word was finally received from the War Department that, yes, in fact, his son John had lost his life in battle.

WILLIAM F. FARRY

The fourth Marblehead casualty was that of William F. Farry, who, according to the telegram delivered to his parents' home on Barnard Street, died in France from bronchial pneumonia on February 6, 1919. He was the son of Thomas and Nellie Ruby Farry and was born on December 31, 1886, in Marblehead.[78] He had left Marblehead on May 31, 1918, for Fort Slocum, New York, and from there was sent to Fort Jackson, South Carolina, serving with the artillery of the Second Corps and going overseas on July 10, 1918. He was a skilled automobile driver and was made a dispatch bearer with a motorcycle. He saw service in the Argonne region and often rode at night through the dark forest carrying dispatches. He was given an automobile to drive, and he and the colonel of this regiment drove through Germany and over a greater part of France.

As upset as William's parents were, they were even more grieved as they did not know exactly where his death occurred or whether he was given his last rites by the chaplain. They had received word from him a short time before that he was soon to set sail for home. As grief-stricken as his mother was, she said that from all the letters she received from William, "he never wrote a sad letter and always tried to paint the situation in bright colors."[79] On the morning following the arrival of the sad news, the remainder of William's company returned by boat to New York; the telegram beat the boat by only about twelve hours.

JOHN MCGEE

John was born on January 5, 1893, in Fitchburg, Massachusetts,[80] the son of James and Mary Donahue McGee. He was married to Evelyn M. Kimball in Marblehead on August 15, 1915.[81] He entered the service on September 20, 1917, in the 76th Division and was transferred on April 27, 1918, to the 301st Infantry, 76th Division. On July 30, 1918, he was again transferred to Company E, 116th Supply Train, 41st Division, and on January 8, 1919, to QMC Detachment, MT Section, Replacement Depot. He went overseas on July 6, 1918. His brother James was also in the service as a first lieutenant in the 315th Infantry, 80th Division. Corporal McGee died February 5, 1919, at Camp Hospital 26, Noyers, France, of disease.[82]

CHRISTIAN SVENE CHRISTENSEN

Christian was born in Mandall, Norway, the son of Salve and Hansine Christensen. He enlisted in the army at the age of twenty-seven, at which time he was living at 11 Nickerson Street in Marblehead. His enlistment date was May 31, 1918, from Swampscott, Massachusetts. He was sent to Camp Jackson, South Carolina, serving in Battery B, 16th Field Artillery, from June 5 to July 11, 1918. He was transferred to Battery D, 129th Field Artillery,

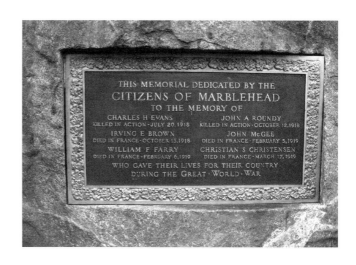

Memorial plaque to those who lost their lives in World War I, Memorial Park, Marblehead. *Photo by Michael Herrick, September 27, 2010, the Historical Marker Database.*

35th Division, and on January 30, 1919, to 273rd MP Company. Christian was transferred overseas and served from July 23, 1918, to March 17, 1919, when he died in France from bronchial pneumonia. He was involved with the following engagements: Vosges Sector; St. Mihiel Offensive; Verdum Sector; and Meuse-Argonne, Defensive Sector.[83]

On Memorial Day 1936, the citizens of town dedicated a bronze plaque set in a large stone at Memorial Park to the memory of all the brave Marbleheaders who "gave their lives for the country during the great war."

Memorial plaque donated by the Live Wire Committee, Memorial Park, Marblehead. *Author's collection.*

ROSTER OF THE TENTH DECK DIVISION

The following is the full roster of men of the Tenth Deck Division as they appear in the full photo on the steps of the post office on Pleasant Street, Marblehead, Massachusetts:

Lieutenant Commander Chester L. Dane and Ensign E.S. Doane

William H. Blackford, William R. Noyes, John Boston, William G. Martin, W. Henry Schofield, Thomas E. Ryan, David O. Snow, John H. Roundy, Howard W. Bartlett, Philip W. Bridgeo, Albert L. Knight, Howard B. Goodwin, Phillip J. Ballard, Frank L. Smith, Percy A. Putnam, Allen D. Weed, Parker Jordan, Frank C. Glass, John W. Clark, Edward T. Lynch, Herman F. Snow, Theodore Bishop, Lawrence M. Mulcahy, Samuel Chapman, Percy L. Martin, Walter A. Washburn, Henry H. Freeto, George E. Lundregan, Ernest Howe, Edmund F. Glover Jr., William Woodfin, Harold W. Woodfin, George Morrill, William Bridgeo, Augustus Shattuck, Ralph P. Graves, Donald A. Snow, Richard L. Feldeman, Willard Harold, John E. Giles, Edward H. Caswell, Frederick C. Jewett, Williard A. Roach, John Q.S. Adams, Herbert G. Dale, Samuel H. Brown, Fred W. Nickerson, William E. Humphrey, William Brown, Russell G. Trefry
Absent from photo: Ensign Lewis Doane, Stephen Rose and Everett Steele

NOTES

Chapter 1

1. *Marblehead Messenger* (hereafter MM), December 3, 1915.
2. Commonwealth of Massachusetts, *Annual Report of the Adjutant General,* year ending December 31, 1916 (n.p.: Wright & Potter Printing Co. State Printers, 1917).
3. en.wikipedia.org/wiki/USS_Kearsarge_(BB-5).
4. *MM*, August 4, 1916.
5. Ibid., September 15, 1916.
6. en.wikipedia.org/wiki/USS_Nebraska_(BB-14).
7. *MM*, April 27, 1917.
8. Ibid., May 4, 1917.
9. Ibid., June 22, 1917.
10. Ibid., October 19, 1917.

Chapter 2

11. en.wikipedia.org/wiki/William_Starling_Burgess.
12. *MM*, July 6, 1917.

Chapter 3

13. Ibid., June 25, 1915.
14. Ibid., November 19, 1915.
15. Ibid., October 19, 1917.
16. Ibid., May 3, 1918.
17. Ibid., February 8, 1918.
18. Ibid., November 19, 1917.
19. Ibid., May 17, 1918.
20. Ibid., June 14, 1918.
21. Ibid., May 18, 1917.
22. Ibid., May 18, 1917.
23. Ibid., June 1, 1917.
24. Ibid., June 8, 1917.
25. Ibid., May 16, 1919.

Chapter 5

26. Ibid., June 7, 1918.
27. Ibid., May 11, 1917.
28. Ibid., April 18, 1918.
29. Ibid., April 19, 1918.

Chapter 6

30. Ibid., June 8, 1917.
31. Ibid., September 28, 1917.
32. Ibid., February 15, 1918.
33. Vital Records, AmericanAncestors.org, Massachusetts Vital Records 1841–1910, Marblehead.
34. Vital Records of Marblehead, Massachusetts, to the end of the year 1976, vol. 2, Marriages: Town Clerk's Office, Marblehead, MA, 1990.
35. *MM*, November 30, 1917.
36. Vital Records of Marblehead, Massachusetts, to the end of the year 1976.

37. Camp Rockingham was the training camp for the Fourteenth Unit of Army Engineers. www.rockinghampark.com.

38. Vital Records, AmericanAncestors.org, Massachusetts Vital Records 1841–1910, Marblehead.

39. Ancestry.com, Social Security Death Index (database online).

40. *MM*, July 18, 1918.

41. Vital Records, AmericanAncestors.org, Massachusetts Vital Records 1841–1910, Marblehead.

42. Ancestry.com, Social Security Death Index (database online).

43. *MM*, July 18, 1918.

44. Vital Records, AmericanAncestors.org, Massachusetts Vital Records 1841–1910, Marblehead.

45. Ancestry.com, Social Security Death Index (database online).

46. *MM*, May 3, 1918.

47. Ibid., August 23, 1918.

48. Ibid., November 1, 1918.

49. Lorraine Allison, "Marblehead in World War I, Part 1," *Marblehead Reporter*, November 23, 1999.

50. Ibid.

51. *MM*, June 21, 1918.

52. Ibid., December 6, 1918.

53. Ibid., November 15, 1918.

CHAPTER 7

54. Ibid., March 1, 1917.

55. Ibid., December 28, 1917.

56. John Harding Peach, *The Peach Tree Handbook, Marblehead Branch*. Vol. 3. Baltimore, MD: Gateway Press, Inc, 2000.

57. *MM*, October 19, 1917.

58. Ibid., October 25, 1918.

Chapter 8

59. Ibid., August 16, 1918.

60. Ibid., July 26, 1918.

61. Vital Records, AmericanAncestors.org, Massachusetts, Vital Records 1841–1910, Marblehead.

62. Vital Records of Marblehead, Massachusetts, to the end of the year 1976.

63. *MM*, April 5, 1918.

64. Ibid., June 7, 1918.

65. Ibid., July 5, 1918.

66. Vital Records, AmericanAncestors.org, Massachusetts Vital Records 1841–1910, Marblehead.

67. Vital Records of Marblehead, Massachusetts, to the end of the year 1976.

68. Military record, Massachusetts National Guard Museum, Worcester, MA.

69. *MM*, March 29, 1918.

70. Ibid., May 3, 1918.

71. Ibid., November 15, 1918.

72. Ibid., January 3, 1919.

73. Vital Records, AmericanAncestors.org, Massachusetts Vital Records 1841–1910, Marblehead.

74. Vital Records of Marblehead, Massachusetts, to the end of the year 1976.

75. *MM*, November 8, 1918.

76. Vital Records, AmericanAncestors.org, Massachusetts Vital Records 1841–1910, Marblehead.

77. Military record, Massachusetts National Guard Museum, Worcester, MA.

78. Vital Records, AmericanAncestors.org, Massachusetts Vital Records 1841–1910, Marblehead.

79. *MM*, February 28, 1919.

80. Vital Records, AmericanAncestors.org, Massachusetts Vital Records 1841–1910, Marblehead.

81. Vital Records of Marblehead, Massachusetts, to the end of the year 1976.

82. Military record, Massachusetts National Guard Museum, Worcester, MA.

83. Ibid.

INDEX

ABOUT THE AUTHOR

Margery Gallo Armstrong is a native Marbleheader, being born and raised there. She has researched her Marblehead family back eleven generations to the early 1600s. Marge has a BS degree from Boston University and recently earned a Certification in Genealogical Research from there. She has been involved in genealogy for the past twelve years and is a member of the Marblehead Historical Society, the Massachusetts Society of Genealogists, the New Hampshire Genealogical Society, the National Society of Genealogists and the New England Genealogical Society. This is her first published work.

Visit us at
www.historypress.net